Success at Its Best: Enhanced Life Skills Curriculum

"Empowering Youth to Excel in Every Aspect of Life"

by Dr. Charmaine Marie, Ed.D.

This curriculum aims to equip youth with the skills necessary for a successful and fulfilling life, and will serve as a comprehensive guide to help youth navigate various aspects of their lives, building a strong foundation for a successful future.

Published by: Real LOVE Publications

Success at Its Best:

Enhanced Life Skills Curriculum

"Empowering Youth to Excel in Every Aspect of Life"

by Dr. Charmaine Marie, Ed.D.

Copyright © 2024 by: Real LOVE Publications.

All rights reserved.

No part of this publication may be reproduced,
stored in a retrieval system or transmitted in any way by any means,
electronic, mechanical, photocopy, recording or otherwise
without the prior permission of the author except
as provided by USA copyright law.

This curriculum is a work of nonfiction. Descriptions,
entities, and incidents included in the story are exclusively
products of the author's imagination. Any resemblance to
events, and entities is entirely coincidental.

ISBN#: 978-1-7377075-6-1

Printed in the United States of America

Table of Contents:

Chapter 1: Character Building

- **Self-Esteem and Loving Yourself Inside and Out**
    - Importance of self-worth
    - Practices for self-love and self-care

Chapter 2: Building Healthy Relationships

- **Identifying Healthy vs. Unhealthy Relationships**
    - Characteristics of supportive relationships
    - Red flags in relationships
    - How to cultivate and maintain healthy relationships

Chapter 3: Goal Setting

- **Setting and Achieving Goals**
    - Steps to set realistic goals
    - Strategies to stay motivated despite obstacles

Chapter 4: Dating Responsibilities

- **Safe and Respectful Dating**
    - Guidelines for healthy dating practices
    - Understanding boundaries and consent

Chapter 5: Understanding STDs

- **Statistics and Prevention**
    - Current statistics on STDs (references from the CDC)
    - What STDs are and their impact on health
    - Abstinence and other prevention methods

Chapter 6: Teenage Pregnancy:

Chapter 7: Introduction to Assertiveness

- **Assertiveness and Boundaries**
  - **Techniques for saying no confidently**
  - **Why it's important to respect your own limits**

Chapter 8: Effective Communication

- **Communicating Assertively and Respectfully**
  - **Tips for effective verbal and non-verbal communication**
  - **Importance of listening and empathy**

Chapter 9: Furthering Your Education

- **Why Education Matters**
  - **Benefits of higher education and vocational training**
  - **Exploring different educational paths**

Chapter 10: Great Hygiene Practices

- **Personal Hygiene and Health**
  - **Daily hygiene routines**
  - **Importance of cleanliness for health and confidence**

Chapter 11: Stop Bullying

- **Recognizing and Responding to Bullying**
  - **Types of bullying and their effects**
  - **Strategies for dealing with bullies**

Chapter 12: Chores and Cleanliness

- **Importance of a Clean Environment**
  - **Responsibilities and benefits of doing chores**
  - **Tips for maintaining a clean living space**

Chapter 13: Financial Stability

- **Managing Your Money Wisely**
    - **Basics of budgeting and saving**
    - **Importance of financial literacy and planning**

Chapter 14: Time Management

- **Using Time Effectively**
    - **Techniques for prioritizing tasks**
    - **Balancing responsibilities and leisure**

Chapter 15: Coping with Stress

- **Healthy Ways to Manage Stress**
    - **Recognizing stress and its sources**
    - **Strategies for stress relief and relaxation**

Chapter 16: Conflict Resolution

- **Handling Conflicts Constructively**
    - **Steps to resolve conflicts peacefully**
    - **Importance of compromise and understanding**

Chapter 17: Civic Responsibility

- **Being an Active and Responsible Citizen**
    - **Importance of community involvement**
    - **Ways to contribute to society positively**

Definitions

References

Chapter 1: Character Building

Section 1: Self-Esteem and Loving Yourself Inside and Out

Content:

- **Define self-esteem and its importance.**
- **Discuss practices for self-love and self-care.**
- **Explore the impact of positive self-talk and affirmations.**

Objective:

To help students understand the importance of self-esteem, self-love, and self-care, and to equip them with tools and practices to foster a positive self-image and maintain mental and emotional well-being.

Activities:

- **Self-Love Journal: Have students create a journal where they write daily positive affirmations and reflections on what they love about themselves.**
- **Compliment Circle: Students sit in a circle and each person gives a compliment to the person next to them, promoting positive reinforcement.**

Understanding Self-Esteem

- **Activity: Start with a group discussion on what students think self-esteem means. Write their definitions on the board.**
- **Definition: Introduce the formal definition of self-esteem as a person's overall sense of their value or worth.**
- **Importance:**
  - **Explain why self-esteem is crucial for mental and emotional health.**
    - **Self-esteem, the perception and evaluation of one's own worth, plays a pivotal role in mental and emotional health. A healthy level of self-esteem contributes to a positive self-image, resilience in the face of challenges, and overall**

psychological well-being. Individuals with high self-esteem are generally more equipped to handle stress, setbacks, and criticism, as they have a strong sense of self-worth and confidence. In contrast, low self-esteem can lead to mental health issues; anxiety, depression, and a strong feeling of inadequacy.

- **Discuss how self-esteem affects behavior, relationships, and success in various aspects of life.**
  - **Behavior:**

    High Self-Esteem: Individuals with high self-esteem tend to exhibit proactive and assertive behaviors. They are more likely to take risks, pursue goals, and express their needs and desires confidently. This positive approach can lead to personal growth and achievement.

    Low Self-Esteem: Those with low self-esteem may exhibit avoidance behaviors, shyness, and a reluctance to take on new challenges. They might also engage in self-sabotaging actions because they do not believe in their own abilities.

  - **Relationships:**

    High Self-Esteem: Healthy self-esteem fosters positive relationships. Individuals with high self-esteem can establish and maintain healthy boundaries, communicate effectively, and form supportive and respectful connections with others. They are also more likely to engage in relationships that are mutually fulfilling.

    Low Self-Esteem: can lead to bad relationships. Individuals may be overly dependent on others for their own validation, tolerate unhealthy or abusive behavior, and struggle with communication. This can result in codependency or chronic conflict within relationships.

  - **Success in Various Aspects of Life:**

    High Self-Esteem: High self-esteem is linked to greater success in academic, professional, and personal endeavors.

Individuals are more likely to set and achieve goals, persist through challenges, and embrace opportunities for growth. Their confidence can inspire others and create a positive feedback loop of success.

Low Self-Esteem: Low self-esteem can hinder success by causing individuals to doubt their capabilities, avoid challenges, and give up easily. This lack of confidence can limit their potential and opportunities, perpetuating a cycle of failure and disappointment.

- Share examples of high vs. low self-esteem.
    - High Self-Esteem:

    A student believes in themselves and their abilities and takes on leadership roles in school clubs, participates actively in class discussions, and is resilient when faced with difficult exams.

    An employee who confidently presents ideas in meetings, seeks out professional development opportunities, and is not afraid to ask for feedback or promotions.

    - Low Self-Esteem:

    A student who avoids participating in class, procrastinates on assignments out of fear of failure, and feels anxious about social interactions with peers.

    An employee who hesitates to share their ideas, avoids challenging tasks, and feels threatened by colleagues' successes, leading to job dissatisfaction and stagnation.

    - Conclusion

    Self-esteem is foundational to mental and emotional health, influencing behavior, relationships, and success across various life domains. Cultivating healthy self-esteem can lead to a more fulfilling, resilient, and successful life, while low self-esteem can pose significant barriers to personal and professional growth. By understanding and nurturing self-esteem, individuals will unlock their full potential and love themselves more, making their lives more meaningful.

Section 2: Practices for Self-Love and Self-Care

Introduction to Self-Love

- **Discussion:** Ask students what self-love means to them and why they think it's important.
- **Definition:** Explain self-love as the practice of taking care of one's own needs and not sacrificing well-being to please others.
- **Benefits:** Discuss the benefits of self-love, such as increased happiness, better relationships, and improved mental health. Self-love has profound benefits on your overall well-being. Here's how embracing self-love can positively impact your life:
  - **Increased Happiness**

    Boosts Self-Esteem: When you practice self-love, you cultivate a positive self-image, which can lead to higher self-esteem and a greater sense of self-worth. This increased confidence often translates into a more joyful and content life.

    Reduces Stress: Loving yourself helps you prioritize self-care, which can reduce stress and increase your ability to enjoy life's moments. You learn to say "no" to things that don't serve you, allowing you to focus on what truly matters.

  - **Better Relationships**

    Healthier Boundaries: Self-love empowers you to set and maintain healthy boundaries in your relationships. This ensures that your interactions are based on mutual respect, leading to more balanced and fulfilling connections.

    Improved Communication: When you love yourself, you're more likely to communicate your needs and desires openly and honestly. This clarity fosters stronger, more authentic relationships with others.

  - **Improved Mental Health**

Reduced Anxiety and Depression: Self-love helps combat negative self-talk and self-criticism, which are often at the root of anxiety and depression. By nurturing a kinder inner dialogue, you can alleviate these mental health challenges.

Increased Resilience: When you love yourself, you become more resilient in the face of adversity and have the ability to cope with life's challenges, as you believe in your own worth and capabilities.

- **Enhanced Personal Growth**

Encourages Self-Reflection: Self-love encourages you to reflect on your strengths and areas for growth without judgment. This self-awareness is key to personal development and achieving your goals.

Motivates Positive Change: When you truly care for yourself, you're more motivated to make positive changes in your life, whether that's pursuing your passions, adopting healthier habits, or seeking new experiences.

- **Greater Overall Well-Being**

Physical Health: Practicing self-love often leads to better physical health, because you may have a desire to exercise regularly, eat healthier, and get more rest.

Life Satisfaction: Ultimately, self-love contributes to a greater sense of life satisfaction. When you accept and appreciate yourself fully, you're more likely to live a life that feels aligned with your true self, bringing you peace and fulfillment.

- **In essence, self-love is the foundation for a happier, healthier, and more fulfilling life. By nurturing your relationship with yourself, you can experience a ripple effect of positivity in all areas of your life.**

Section 3: Positive Self-Talk and Affirmations

Understanding Positive Self-Talk

- **Definition:** Explain positive self-talk as the practice of speaking to oneself in an encouraging and supportive manner.
- **Impact:** Discuss how positive self-talk can improve self-esteem and overall outlook on life.
- **Examples:** Share examples of negative vs. positive self-talk and their potential effects.
    - **Negative Self-Talk Examples**

        "I can't do anything right."

        > **Effect:** This statement can lead to feelings of incompetence and helplessness, reducing motivation to try new things.

        "I'm not good enough for this job."

        > **Effect:** Such thoughts can undermine self-esteem and result in poor performance at work due to lack of confidence.

        "I'll never be able to lose weight."

        > **Effect:** This mindset can discourage efforts towards healthy living and lead to feelings of defeat and frustration.

        "No one likes me."

        > **Effect:** Believing this can cause social withdrawal and loneliness, exacerbating feelings of isolation.

    - **Positive Self-Talk Examples**

        "I can learn from my mistakes."

        > **Effect:** This encourages displaying mistakes as opportunities to learning, grow, and be better.

        "I am capable and competent."

> **Effect:** Such affirmations build self-esteem and foster a sense of competence, leading to better performance and achievements.

> **"I am making progress towards my goals."**

> **Effect:** This positive reinforcement can motivate continued effort and perseverance, enhancing goal attainment.

> **"I am valued and appreciated."**

> **Effect:** Feeling valued boosts self-worth and promotes positive relationships with others, contributing to a sense of belonging.

- **By consciously practicing positive self-talk, you can transform your mindset, improve your self-esteem, and foster a more optimistic outlook on life.**

Section 4: Creating Affirmations

- **Activity: Guide students in creating their own affirmations.**
- **Practice: Have students write down three affirmations they can use daily.**
- **Group Sharing: Allow students to share their affirmations with the class if they feel comfortable.**

By the end of this chapter, students should have a solid understanding of self-esteem, practical tools for self-love and self-care, and the ability to implement positive self-talk and affirmations in their daily lives.

Worksheet 1: Understanding Self-Esteem and Positive Self-Talk

Part 1: What is Self-Esteem?

1. **Define Self-Esteem:**
    o In your own words, write down what self-esteem means to you.

    _____
    _____
    _____

2. **Self-Esteem Importance:**
    o Why is self-esteem important for your mental and emotional health? Write at least two reasons.

    _____
    _____

3. **High vs. Low Self-Esteem:**
    o Provide an example of behavior that someone with high self-esteem might exhibit.
    o Provide an example of behavior that someone with low self-esteem might exhibit.

High Self-Esteem Example:

_____
_____

Low Self-Esteem Example:

_____
_____

Part 2: Positive Self-Talk

1. **Understanding Positive Self-Talk:**
    - Write a negative self-talk statement you might sometimes think.
    - Rewrite this statement as a positive self-talk affirmation.

Negative Self-Talk:
_____

Positive Self-Talk:
_____

2. **Creating Your Own Affirmations:**
    - Write down three positive affirmations you can use daily to boost your self-esteem.

_____

_____

_____

_____

Worksheet 2: Self-Love and Self-Care Practices

Part 1: What is Self-Love?

1. **Define Self-Love:**
    - Write down what self-love means to you.

   _____

   _____

2. **Benefits of Self-Love:**
    - List three benefits of practicing self-love.

   _____

   _____

   _____

Part 2: Self-Love Journal Activity

1. **Daily Affirmations:**
    - Write three things you love about yourself today.

   _____

   _____

   _____

2. **Reflection:**
    - Reflect on how practicing self-love made you feel today. Write a few sentences.

   _____

   _____

Chapter 2: Building Healthy Relationships

Section 1: Identifying Healthy vs. Unhealthy Relationships

Content:

- **Introduction to Relationships**
- **Characteristics of supportive and toxic relationships.**
- **Importance of trust, respect, and communication in relationships.**
- **Strategies to build and maintain healthy relationships.**

Definition of relationships (family, friends, romantic, professional)

- **Family Relationships:**
  - **Definition: These are connections formed between individuals who are related by blood, marriage, or adoption. They include parent-child relationships, sibling relationships, and extended family relationships such as those with grandparents, aunts, uncles, and cousins.**
  - **Characteristics: Typically long-lasting and foundational, providing emotional support, cultural identity, and a sense of belonging.**

- **Friend Relationships:**
  - **Definition: Voluntary connections formed between individuals based on mutual affection, shared interests, or common experiences. These relationships are not bound by family ties or professional obligations.**
  - **Characteristics: Often characterized by trust, companionship, and emotional support, friends can offer a sense of belonging and community.**

- **Romantic Relationships:**
  - **Definition: Intimate relationships involving emotional and physical connection, often characterized by love, affection,**

and sexual attraction. These relationships can be between partners who are dating, cohabiting, or married.

- Characteristics: Typically involve a deep emotional bond, shared goals and values, and mutual support. They can be a significant source of personal fulfillment and happiness.

- **Professional Relationships:**
  - Definition: Connections formed between individuals in a work or professional context. These relationships include those with colleagues, supervisors, subordinates, clients, and business partners.
  - Characteristics: Often goal-oriented and based on mutual respect and collaboration. Professional relationships can enhance career growth, provide networking opportunities, and contribute to a productive work environment.=

- The role of relationships in personal growth and well-being
  - **Emotional Support:**

    Relationships provide a network of support during times of stress, grief, or hardship. Family and friends offer a safe space to express emotions, seek advice, and find comfort, which is crucial for mental health.

  - **Sense of Belonging:**

    Feeling connected to others fosters a sense of belonging and community. This can enhance self-esteem and reduce feelings of loneliness and isolation, which are important for emotional well-being.

  - **Personal Development:**

    Relationships can challenge individuals to grow and improve. Constructive feedback from family, friends, and colleagues can help one to hone in on their strengths and areas for personal and professional growth.

  - **Learning and Inspiration:**

> Interacting with diverse individuals exposes one to different perspectives, ideas, and experiences. This can inspire creativity, broaden horizons, and promote lifelong learning.

- **Stress Reduction:**

  Having supportive relationships can buffer against stress. The presence of loved ones can reduce cortisol levels and promote relaxation, contributing to overall physical health.

- **Health Benefits:**

  Positive relationships are linked to numerous health benefits, including lower blood pressure, improved immune function, and longer lifespan. Emotional support from relationships leads to healthier life choices.

- **Career Advancement:**

  Professional relationships offer new opportunities, mentorship, and career advancement. Networking and collaboration with colleagues can lead to skill development and job satisfaction.

- **Happiness and Fulfillment:**

  Strong, positive relationships are a significant source of joy and satisfaction. Celebrating successes, sharing experiences, and building memories with loved ones contribute to a fulfilling life.

- In conclusion, relationships play a vital role in personal growth and well-being by providing emotional support, fostering a sense of belonging, encouraging personal development, reducing stress, offering health benefits, enhancing career prospects, and contributing to overall happiness and fulfillment.

Section 2: Characteristics of Supportive and Toxic Relationships

Ask students the characteristics of a supportive/healthy relationship

- Supportive Relationships
  - Mutual Respect:

- Definition: Valuing each other's opinions, feelings, and boundaries.
- Characteristics: In a mutually respectful relationship, individuals listen to each other, appreciate their differences, and avoid belittling or dismissing each other's thoughts and feelings.

- Trust:
  - Definition: Believing in the reliability, honesty, and integrity of the other person.
  - Characteristics: Trustworthy relationships involve being honest, keeping promises, and feeling secure in the knowledge that the other person has your best interests at heart.

- Open Communication:
  - Definition: Sharing thoughts, feelings, and concerns openly and honestly.
  - Characteristics: In relationships with open communication, individuals feel comfortable expressing themselves without fear of judgment or retribution. They actively listen and respond thoughtfully.

- Empathy:
  - Definition: Understanding and sharing the feelings of another person.
  - Characteristics: Empathetic relationships involve showing compassion, validating each other's feelings, and being supportive during difficult times.

- Encouragement:
  - Definition: Providing support and motivation to help each other grow and succeed.

- Characteristics: Encouraging relationships involve offering praise, celebrating achievements, and being a source of positivity and strength for one another.
- **Healthy Boundaries:**
    - Definition: Recognizing and respecting each other's personal space and limits.
    - Characteristics: In relationships with healthy boundaries, individuals understand the importance of personal time, privacy, and the need to say no when necessary without feeling guilty.

Ask students the characteristics of an unsupportive/unhealthy relationship

- **Toxic Relationships**
    - **Manipulation:**
        - Definition: Influencing someone unfairly or dishonestly to gain control or advantage.
        - Characteristics: Manipulative relationships involve deceit, guilt-tripping, and pressure tactics to make the other person act in a desired way, often against their own best interests.
    - **Lack of Trust:**
        - Definition: Doubting the honesty, integrity, or reliability of the other person.
        - Characteristics: In relationships with a lack of trust, individuals may experience constant suspicion, jealousy, and the need to verify the other person's actions and intentions frequently.
    - **Poor Communication:**
        - Definition: Ineffective or harmful exchange of thoughts and feelings.
        - Characteristics: Poor communication in relationships involves frequent misunderstandings, lack of listening,

avoidance of important discussions, and unresolved conflicts.

- **Disrespect:**
    - **Definition: Failing to show consideration or appreciation for the other person.**
    - **Characteristics: Disrespectful relationships involve insults, belittling, dismissiveness, and ignoring the other person's opinions and needs.**

- **Control:**
    - **Definition: Dominating or regulating the other person's behavior, decisions, and actions.**
    - **Characteristics: Controlling relationships involve dictating what the other person can or cannot do, making unilateral decisions, and restricting their freedom and autonomy.**

- **Jealousy:**
    - **Definition: Feeling insecure or threatened by the other person's interactions or relationships with others.**
    - **Characteristics: Jealous relationships involve constant accusations, demands for reassurance, and attempts to isolate the other person from friends and family.**

This chapter aims to provide students with a comprehensive understanding of healthy versus unhealthy relationships, the importance of key elements like trust, respect, and communication, and practical strategies for fostering and maintaining healthy relationships. Through discussions, activities, and assessments, students will gain the skills and knowledge necessary to build supportive and meaningful connections.

Worksheet 1: Identifying Characteristics of Healthy vs. Unhealthy Relationships

Part 1: Matching Activity Match each characteristic with the type of relationship it best describes. Write the letter of the correct type of relationship next to each characteristic.

Relationship Types:

    A. Supportive Relationship
    B. Toxic Relationship

Characteristics:

1. ____ Trust: Believing in the reliability, honesty, and integrity of the other person.

2. ____ Manipulation: Influencing someone unfairly to gain control or advantage.

3. ____ Empathy: Understanding and sharing the feelings of another person.

4. ____ Lack of Trust: Constant suspicion and doubt about the other person's honesty.

5. ____ Healthy Boundaries: Respecting each other's personal space and limits.

6. ____ Poor Communication: Ineffective exchange of thoughts and feelings.

7. ____ Mutual Respect: Valuing each other's opinions, feelings, and boundaries.

8. ____ Control: Dominating or regulating the other person's behavior and actions.

Part 2: Short Answer

1. What are three characteristics of a supportive relationship?

    o _____

    o _____

    o _____

2. What are two signs that a relationship might be toxic?

    o _____

    o _____

Part 3: Reflection Think about a relationship in your life (family, friend, romantic, or professional). Without naming the person, describe whether you believe this relationship is more supportive or toxic and why.

- _____

- _____

- _____

Worksheet 2: Building and Maintaining Healthy Relationships

Part 1: Definition Matching Match each definition with the correct type of relationship. Write the letter of the correct relationship type next to each definition.

Relationship Types:

    A. Family Relationship
    B. Friend Relationship
    C. Romantic Relationship
    D. Professional Relationship

Definitions:

1. ____ Connections formed between individuals in a work context, focused on mutual respect and collaboration.

2. ____ Voluntary connections formed based on mutual affection, shared interests, or experiences.

3. ____ Intimate relationships involving emotional and physical connection, often characterized by love and affection.

4. ____ Connections formed between individuals related by blood, marriage, or adoption.

Part 2: Fill in the Blank Fill in the blanks using the word bank below.

Word Bank:

- **Emotional Support**
- **Sense of Belonging**
- **Trust**
- **Open Communication**
- **Encouragement**

1. _____ is the foundation of any healthy relationship, allowing individuals to feel safe and secure.

2. A strong _____ can help reduce feelings of loneliness and enhance self-esteem.

3. _____ involves sharing thoughts and feelings openly and honestly with one another.

4. Offering _____ during difficult times is essential to providing emotional support.

5. Celebrating each other's successes and offering _____ can strengthen any relationship.

Part 3: Scenario Analysis Read the following scenario and answer the questions.

Scenario:
Alex and Jamie have been friends for several years. Recently, Jamie has noticed that Alex often interrupts him during conversations, dismisses his opinions, and sometimes pressures him to do things he doesn't want to do. Jamie feels uncomfortable but doesn't want to lose the friendship.

1. Based on the characteristics discussed, would you consider Alex and Jamie's relationship supportive or toxic? Explain your answer.

    o _____
    o _____

2. What are two strategies Jamie could use to address the issues in their relationship?

    o _____
    o _____

3. If you were Jamie's friend, what advice would you give him?

    o _____
    o _____

Chapter 3: Goal Setting

Section 1: Setting and Achieving Goals

Goal Setting

The process of identifying measurable and achievable objectives that guide actions and decisions. This process involves defining clear outcomes and establishing a plan to achieve them, serving as a roadmap for personal and professional development.

The Importance of Having Goals

- **Direction and Focus:** Goals provide a clear direction, helping to concentrate efforts and resources on achieving desired outcomes.

- **Motivation and Commitment:** Goals inspire motivation, providing a sense of purpose and driving persistent effort.

- **Measurable Progress:** Having specific goals allows for tracking progress and celebrating milestones, which fosters continuous improvement.

- **Decision Making:** Goals serve as a framework for making informed decisions that align with desired outcomes.

- **Personal Growth:** Setting and pursuing goals encourages personal and professional growth, pushing individuals to develop new skills and expand their capabilities.

Types of Goals

- **Short-Term Goals:** Objectives that can be achieved in a relatively short period, usually within a year. They provide immediate direction and quick wins.
  - Example: Completing a certification course within six months.

- **Long-Term Goals:** Objectives that require a longer time to achieve, typically spanning several years. They offer a vision for the future.
  - Example: Saving for retirement or earning a college degree.

- **Personal Goals:** Goals related to personal development, health, relationships, hobbies, and overall well-being.

- Example: Exercising regularly or reading a certain number of books per year.
- **Professional Goals:** Goals related to career advancement, skills development, and professional achievements.
  - Example: Achieving a promotion or mastering a new technology relevant to your job.

Section 2: Steps to Set Realistic and Achievable Goals

Your Vision: What do you want to achieve?

Set SMART Goals:

- **Specific:** Clearly define the goal, including the what, why, and how.
- **Measurable:** Set up a criteria to measure your progress.
- **Achievable:** Be sure that your goals realistic and attainable.
- **Relevant:** Align your goal with your big picture of your objectives and values.
- **Time-Bound:** Always have a deadline for achieving your goals.

Put Your Goals into Achievable Steps: Create smaller manageable tasks out of larger goals to make the process more attainable.

Create a Plan: Develop a detailed action plan, including timelines, resources needed, and potential obstacles.

Keep Track of Your Progress: Do daily and weekly reviews of all of your work to assure you stay on track.

Section 3: Importance of Planning and Persistence

Planning: A well-thought-out plan provides a clear roadmap to follow, helping to anticipate challenges and allocate resources effectively. It ensures that efforts are focused and organized.

Persistence: Staying committed to your goals despite setbacks is crucial. Persistence involves maintaining motivation, adapting to changes, and continuously striving toward your objectives.

Section 4: Overcoming Obstacles and Staying Motivated

Identify Potential Obstacles:

- **Lack of time**
- **Limited resources**
- **Personal setbacks (e.g., illness, family issues)**
- **External factors (e.g., school workload, peer pressure)**

Be Flexible: Be open to adjusting your plan. Flexibility is key.

Seek Support: Surround yourself with supportive individuals who can provide encouragement, advice, and accountability.

Celebrate Small Wins: Recognize and celebrate progress to ensure you maintain motivation and build momentum.

Maintain a Positive Mindset: Focus on the positive aspects of your journey and learn from setbacks rather than becoming discouraged.

By following these steps and maintaining a focus on planning and persistence, you can effectively set and achieve your goals, overcome obstacles, and stay motivated while you create success for yourself.

Worksheet 1: Understanding Goal Setting

Section 1: Goal Setting Concepts

1. Define Goal Setting:
In your own words, describe what goal setting means and why it is important.

_____

_____

2. Types of Goals:
Match the following types of goals with their examples:

<u>Type of Goal</u>   <u>Example</u>

Short-Term Goal   A. Saving for retirement

Long-Term Goal   B. Exercising three times a week for the next month

Personal Goal   C. Completing a course in six months

Professional Goal D. Earning a college degree

3. Benefits of Goal Setting:
List three benefits of setting goals and briefly explain how each can impact your life.

  1. _____
  2. _____
  3. _____

4. Reflection:
Think about a goal you have set in the past. Was it short-term or long-term? Did you achieve it? What helped or hindered your progress?

_____

_____

Worksheet 2: Setting SMART Goals

Section 2: Steps to Set Realistic and Achievable Goals

1. Your Vision:
Write down a vision of what you want to achieve in the next year. It can be related to school, a hobby, or any personal goal.

_____

2. Set a SMART Goal:
Using the vision you wrote down, break it down into a SMART goal. Fill in the blanks below:

- Specific: What exactly do you want to achieve?

  _____

- Measurable: How will you know when you've achieved it?

  _____

- Achievable: Is your goal realistic? What resources or skills will you need?

  _____

- Relevant: How does this goal align with your larger objectives?

  _____

- Time-Bound: What is your deadline for achieving this goal?

  _____

3. Breaking Down the Goal:
List three smaller steps you can take to achieve your SMART goal.

1. _____
2. _____
3. _____

Chapter 4: Dating Responsibilities

Section 1: Introduction to Safe and Respectful Dating –

Dating responsibilities refer to the behaviors and actions individuals must take to ensure their dating relationships are healthy, respectful, and safe for both partners.

Mutual Respect and Trust :

- Mutual respect involves treating your partner with consideration and valuing their feelings and opinions.
    - Trust is foundational to any relationship, allowing partners to feel secure and supported.
    - **Healthy Dating Practices:**
- Encourages open communication, honesty, and shared interests.
- Promotes equal power dynamics and decision-making.
- Listen
- Express your feelings and needs clearly.

- **Respect:**
    - Show respect for your partner's opinions, feelings, and boundaries.
    - Treat each other with kindness and consideration.

- **Equality:**
    - Ensure decisions in the relationship are made jointly.
    - Avoid controlling or dominating behaviors.

Consent and Boundaries:

- Understanding that consent is a clear, enthusiastic, and ongoing agreement between partners. Consent must be given freely, enthusiastically, and can be withdrawn at any time.
- Discuss clearly and agree on physical and emotional boundaries with your partner and respect your partner's boundaries.

Quick Review:

Dating Do's and Don'ts

Do's:

- Communicate openly and honestly.
- Show respect for each other's feelings and opinions.
- Establish and respect personal boundaries.
- Spend quality time together and apart.

Don'ts:

- Don't pressure your partner into doing something they are uncomfortable with.
- Don't engage in controlling or manipulative behavior.
- Don't ignore signs of abuse or disrespect.
- Don't compromise your values or boundaries for the sake of the relationship.

Section 2: Warning Signs of Unhealthy/Abusive Relationships

Red flags include:

- **Extreme Jealousy or Possessiveness:** A partner constantly accuses you of cheating or being unfaithful.
- **Controlling Behavior:** They dictate what you can and cannot do, who you can see, where you can go, and what you can wear.
- **Quick Involvement:** The relationship progresses very quickly, with intense declarations of love and demands for exclusivity early on.
- **Isolation:** Your partner tries to cut you off from friends, family, and other support systems.
- **Verbal Insults:** Frequent use of derogatory language, name-calling, and demeaning comments.

- **Blame-Shifting:** They never take responsibility for their actions and always blame you for their abusive behavior.
- **Mood Swings:** Your partner has unpredictable and extreme mood changes, often going from very loving to abusive quickly.
- **Threats and Intimidation:** They use threats of violence, self-harm, or harm to loved ones to control or manipulate you.

Section 3: Recognizing Dating Violence:

- Look out for signs of controlling behavior, verbal abuse, physical aggression, and manipulation.
- Understand that abuse can be emotional, psychological, or physical.
- Knowing how to seek help and support if experiencing or witnessing dating violence.
- If you or someone you know is experiencing dating violence, seek help from a trusted adult, counselor, or support service.
- Develop a safety plan and know resources available for victims of dating violence.

Section 4: Dating violence can manifest in several forms, including:

- **Physical Abuse:** Involves any use of physical force against a partner, such as hitting, slapping, punching, kicking, or choking.
- **Emotional Abuse:** Includes behaviors that undermine an individual's sense of self-worth or self-esteem, such as constant criticism, manipulation, humiliation, and isolation from friends and family.
- **Verbal Abuse:** Entails the use of words to harm or control a partner, including yelling, insulting, belittling, and threatening.
- **Sexual Abuse:** Involves any forced or coerced sexual activity, including rape, unwanted touching, and pressuring a partner into sexual acts they are uncomfortable with.

Section 5: Resources and Support Systems: Where to Seek Help

If you or someone you know is experiencing dating violence, there are various resources and support systems available:

- **National Domestic Violence Hotline:** Call 1-800-799-SAFE (7233) for confidential support and resources.

- **Local Shelters and Support Services:** Many communities have shelters, counseling services, and support groups for individuals experiencing domestic violence.

- **School Counselors and Trusted Adults:** Reach out to a trusted teacher, school counselor, or other adult who can provide support and guide you to appropriate resources.

- **Law Enforcement:** If you are in immediate danger, call 911 or your local emergency number.

Section 6: Strategies for Safely Ending an Abusive Relationship

Ending an abusive relationship can be challenging and requires careful planning to ensure safety:

- **Create a Safety Plan:** Develop a detailed plan that includes safe places to go, people to contact, and steps to take in case of an emergency.

- **Inform Trusted Individuals:** Let friends, family, or trusted adults know about your situation and plan to leave, so they can provide support and assistance.

- **Avoid Confrontation:** If possible, avoid breaking up with the abuser in person. Opt for a phone call, text, or a letter to maintain a safe distance.

- **Change Your Routine:** Alter your daily habits and routes to avoid encounters with your ex-partner.

- **Secure Your Communications:** Change passwords and ensure that your phone and social media accounts are secure to prevent the abuser from tracking or contacting you.

- **Legal Protection:** Consider obtaining a restraining order or protective order to legally prevent the abuser from contacting or approaching you.
- **Seek Professional Help:** Talk to a counselor or principal for guidance.

By recognizing the types and signs of dating violence, knowing where to seek help, and understanding how to safely end an abusive relationship, individuals can take steps for protection and a healthier future.

Worksheet 1: Understanding Safe and Respectful Dating

Part 1: Key Concepts Matching Match the term with the correct definition.

1. Mutual Respect
2. Trust
3. Consent
4. Boundaries
5. Equality

a) An agreement that is clear, enthusiastic, ongoing, and can be withdrawn at any time.
b) Treating your partner with consideration and valuing their feelings and opinions.
c) Ensuring that both partners have an equal say in decision-making and avoid dominating behaviors.
d) Understanding and agreeing on the limits in a relationship, both physical and emotional.
e) The foundation of a relationship that allows partners to feel secure and supported.

Part 2: Healthy vs. Unhealthy Dating Practices

Below are examples of dating behaviors. Write "Healthy" or "Unhealthy" next to each one.

1. Encouraging your partner to spend time with their friends and family.
2. Pressuring your partner to spend all their time with you.
3. Listening to your partner's feelings and concerns.
4. Ignoring your partner's boundaries.
5. Making decisions together about your relationship.
6. Calling your partner names during an argument.
7. Respecting your partner's need for personal space.

8. Blaming your partner for your mistakes.

Part 3: Scenario Analysis

Read the following scenarios and answer the questions.

Scenario 1:
Alex and Jordan have been dating for a few months. Jordan often checks Alex's phone without asking and gets upset when Alex talks to other people, even friends.

- Is this behavior respectful and healthy? Why or why not?
- What could Alex do to address this issue?

Scenario 2:
Taylor and Morgan always discuss their weekend plans together and make sure they both agree on what to do. They listen to each other's opinions and make decisions as a team.

- How does this scenario demonstrate mutual respect and equality in the relationship?
- Why are these practices important in a healthy relationship?

Worksheet 2: Recognizing and Responding to Unhealthy Relationships

Part 1: Identifying Red Flags

Circle the behaviors that are red flags of an unhealthy or abusive relationship.

- Frequent mood swings from very loving to abusive
- Sharing personal information only with mutual consent
- Demanding to know your location at all times
- Encouraging your partner to pursue their hobbies
- Isolating you from friends and family
- Making you feel guilty for spending time apart
- Listening to your partner's opinions
- Pressuring you into making decisions quickly

Part 2: Role-Playing Exercise

For this exercise, pair up with a classmate. One of you will play the role of a friend who is concerned about their friend's relationship, and the other will play the person experiencing unhealthy behavior in their relationship.

- **Scenario:** Your friend mentions that their partner has started controlling who they can hang out with and often criticizes them in public.
- **Discussion Questions:**
    - What would you say to your friend to express your concern?
    - How can you support your friend if they want to leave the relationship?
    - What resources or steps could your friend take to ensure their safety?

Part 3: Creating a Safety Plan

Imagine you or a friend is in an unhealthy relationship. Write down a safety plan including:

1. **Trusted Individuals:** List three people you would reach out to for support.

2. **Safe Places:** Identify two places you could go if you need to leave quickly.

3. **Emergency Steps:** Outline the steps you would take in case of an emergency, such as contacting the authorities or going to a shelter.

4. **Communication Security:** What steps would you take to secure your phone and social media accounts?

Part 4: Reflection

Write a short reflection on why it is important to recognize the signs of dating violence and know how to seek help. Include how you can apply this knowledge in your own life or help a friend in need.

Chapter 5: Understanding STDs - Statistics and Prevention

Section 1: Overview of STDs

- **Bacterial STDs:** Chlamydia, Gonorrhea, Syphilis
- **Viral STDs:** Human Immunodeficiency Virus (HIV), Herpes Simplex Virus (HSV), Human Papillomavirus (HPV)
- **Parasitic STDs:** Trichomoniasis

Current Statistics on STDs

- Chlamydia
    - Current Statistics:
        - In 2022, there were approximately 1.7 million reported cases of chlamydia in the United States (CDC).
        - Chlamydia is the most commonly reported STD.
        - Highest rates are among females aged 15-24 and males aged 20-24.
    - Impact:
        - Can lead to pelvic inflammatory disease (PID) and infertility if untreated.
        - Often asymptomatic, especially in women.
- Gonorrhea
    - Current Statistics:
        - In 2022, there were about 700,000 cases of gonorrhea reported in the United States (CDC).
        - Rates are highest among males aged 20-24 and females aged 15-24.
    - Impact:

- Can cause serious health problems like PID and increase susceptibility to HIV.
- Symptoms include painful urination and discharge, but many people are asymptomatic.

- Syphilis
    - Current Statistics:
        - In 2022, over 170,000 cases of syphilis were reported (CDC).
        - The number of congenital syphilis cases is also rising, with over 2,500 cases reported in 2022.
        - Highest rates among men who have sex with men (MSM).
    - Impact:
        - Can cause long-term health issues if untreated, including cardiovascular and neurological problems.
        - Syphilis has stages (primary, secondary, latent, and tertiary) with varying symptoms.

- Herpes Simplex Virus (HSV)
    - Current Statistics:
        - An estimated 1 in 6 people aged 14-49 in the U.S. has genital herpes (CDC).
        - About 500,000 new cases annually.
    - Impact:
        - Causes painful sores and can lead to recurrent outbreaks.
        - No cure, but antiviral medications can manage symptoms.

- Human Papillomavirus (HPV)
    - Current Statistics:
        - HPV is the most common sexually transmitted infection. Nearly all sexually active people will contract HPV at some point.

- In 2022, over 40,000 cases of HPV-related cancers were reported in the U.S. (CDC).
- Impact:
  - Most HPV infections are asymptomatic and clear up on their own.
  - Some types can cause genital warts or lead to cancers such as cervical cancer.
- HIV/AIDS
  - Current Statistics:
    - Approximately 1.2 million people in the U.S. are living with HIV (CDC).
    - In 2022, about 35,000 new HIV diagnoses were reported.
    - Highest rates among MSM and African American communities.
  - Impact:
    - HIV progresses to AIDS if untreated, leading to severe immune system damage and increased susceptibility to infections.
    - Antiretroviral therapy (ART) can manage HIV effectively, allowing individuals to live long, healthy lives.
- Trichomoniasis
  - Current Statistics:
    - An estimated 3.7 million people in the U.S. have trichomoniasis (CDC).
    - More common in women than men.
  - Impact:
    - Can cause discomfort and increase susceptibility to other STDs, including HIV.

Section 2: Condom Use Statistics

- **Current Statistics:**
  - Approximately 75% of sexually active individuals report using condoms consistently (National Center for Health Statistics).
  - Condom use has been shown to reduce the risk of STDs and unintended pregnancies by up to 80%.
- **Effectiveness:**
  - Proper use of condoms is highly effective in reducing the transmission of STDs and preventing pregnancies.
  - Latex condoms are most effective, but other types (e.g., polyurethane) are also available for individuals with latex allergies.

Section 3: Teenage Pregnancy Statistics

- **Current Statistics:**
  - In 2022, the U.S. had a teenage birth rate of about 15.3 births per 1,000 females aged 15-19 (CDC).
  - Significant declines in teenage pregnancy rates have been observed over the past decades.
- **Impact:**
  - Teen pregnancies can lead to health risks for both the mother and child.
  - Often associated with lower educational attainment and economic challenges.

Demographic Breakdown

- **Age Groups**
  - STDs are more prevalent among younger individuals, particularly those aged 15-24.
  - The highest rates of chlamydia and gonorrhea are observed in this age group.
- **Gender**

- Females are more likely to be diagnosed with chlamydia and gonorrhea compared to males.
- Males are more likely to be diagnosed with syphilis, especially among MSM.
- **Sexual Orientation**
    - MSM are at higher risk for STDs like syphilis and HIV.
    - Higher prevalence of STDs among individuals with multiple sexual partners.
- **Race and Ethnicity**
    - Higher rates of STDs are observed in African American and Hispanic communities.
    - Disparities are attributed to various factors, including access to healthcare and socioeconomic conditions.
- **Geographical Variation**
    - Urban areas generally report higher rates of STDs compared to rural areas.
    - Regional differences in STD rates can be influenced by local healthcare access and prevention programs.

Prevention Methods

- **Abstinence**
    - Emphasize abstinence as the only 100% effective method for preventing STDs.
    - Encourage open discussions about the benefits of abstinence in various educational settings.
- **Condom Use**
    - Educate on proper condom use and availability.
    - Highlight the importance of using condoms consistently and correctly to prevent STDs and unintended pregnancies.
- **Regular Testing**

- **Promote the importance of routine STD screenings, particularly for sexually active individuals.**
- **Provide information on where to get tested and the benefits of early detection.**
- **Vaccinations**
  - **HPV has a vaccine.**
- **Mutual Monogamy**
  - **To prevent STDs someone should be in a single, mutually monogamous partner who has been tested and is STD-free.**
- **Education and Communication**
  - **It is important to have open communication about sexual health with partners.**

This detailed curriculum aims to provide a thorough understanding of STDs, their impact, and effective prevention strategies.

Worksheet 1: Understanding STDs – Comprehension and Statistics

Section 1: Matching Exercise
Match the following STDs with their corresponding description or statistic:

1. Chlamydia
2. Gonorrhea
3. Syphilis
4. Herpes Simplex Virus (HSV)
5. Human Papillomavirus (HPV)
6. HIV/AIDS
7. Trichomoniasis

a. Involves stages and can lead to cardiovascular and neurological problems if untreated.
b. The most common sexually transmitted infection, often asymptomatic but can lead to cancer.
c. Can cause painful sores with recurrent outbreaks but is manageable with antiviral medications.
d. In 2022, there were approximately 1.7 million reported cases in the U.S., often asymptomatic, especially in women.
e. Approximately 1.2 million people in the U.S. are living with this, and without treatment, it can lead to severe immune system damage.
f. An estimated 3.7 million people in the U.S. have this parasitic STD, more common in women.
g. Rates are highest among males aged 20-24 and females aged 15-24, with symptoms including painful urination and discharge.

Section 2: Short Answer

1. What are the three main categories of STDs?

2. Explain why STDs like chlamydia and gonorrhea are often underreported.

3. What is the significance of the demographic breakdown in understanding STD prevalence?

4. Why is it important to get regular STD screenings, even if you don't show symptoms?

Section 3: Statistics Interpretation

Review the following statistics and answer the questions:

- In 2022, the U.S. reported approximately 700,000 cases of gonorrhea.
- There were about 170,000 cases of syphilis reported.
- An estimated 1 in 6 people aged 14-49 in the U.S. has genital herpes (HSV).

1. Based on the statistics above, which STD is more prevalent in the U.S., and why might this be the case?

2. Discuss the potential impact of these statistics on public health initiatives.

Worksheet 2: STD Prevention and Awareness

Section 1: Multiple Choice

1. Which of the following is NOT a bacterial STD?
   a. Chlamydia
   b. Gonorrhea
   c. Herpes Simplex Virus (HSV)
   d. Syphilis

2. What is the most effective method for preventing STDs?
   a. Consistent condom use
   b. Abstinence
   c. Mutual monogamy
   d. Regular testing

3. Which demographic group is at the highest risk for chlamydia?
   a. Males aged 30-35

4. b. Females aged 15-24
   c. Individuals aged 40-49
   d. Females aged 50-60

5. What percentage of sexually active individuals report using condoms consistently?
   a. 50%
   b. 60%
   c. 75%
   d. 85%

Section 2: True or False

1. HPV has a vaccine that can prevent certain types of infections.

2. Trichomoniasis is more common in men than in women.

3. Regular testing is only necessary if you experience symptoms of an STD.

4. Syphilis can only be spread through sexual contact.

Section 3: Scenario-Based Questions

Scenario 1: Consent and Communication
Alex and Jordan have been dating for a few months. They are thinking about becoming sexually active but want to ensure they are both safe and healthy.

1. What steps should Alex and Jordan take to prevent the transmission of STDs?//
2. How can they communicate about their sexual health and boundaries effectively?

Scenario 2: Identifying and Addressing Risk
Taylor is in a new relationship and is unsure if they should get tested for STDs. Taylor's partner has mentioned that they have never been tested.

1. What advice would you give Taylor regarding STD testing?
2. Why is it important for both partners to be informed about each other's sexual health?

Section 4: Reflection

Reflect on what you've learned about STDs and prevention. Write a short paragraph on how you can apply this knowledge in your own life or to help others.

Chapter 6: Teenage Pregnancy: Statistics, Demographics, and Prevention

Section 1: Teenage pregnancy remains a critical issue that impacts individuals, families, and communities. This chapter explores the statistics and demographics associated with teenage pregnancy and provides insights into effective prevention strategies to address this challenge.

Teenage pregnancy rates have fluctuated over the years, reflecting changes in societal attitudes, access to education, and healthcare resources. As of the latest available data:

- **Prevalence:** According to the Centers for Disease Control and Prevention (CDC), the teen birth rate in the United States has seen a significant decline in recent years. In 2023, the birth rate for females aged 15-19 was approximately 15.1 births per 1,000 women, a notable decrease from previous decades.

- **Age Trends:** Most teenage pregnancies occur in older teens, with the majority of births to mothers aged 18-19, compared to those aged 15-17.

- **Ethnic and Racial Disparities:** Data indicates that teenage pregnancy rates vary by ethnicity. Hispanic and Black teenagers have historically had higher rates of pregnancy compared to their White counterparts. Efforts to address these disparities involve culturally tailored education and support programs.

- **Socioeconomic Factors:** Teenage pregnancy rates are higher among individuals from low-income backgrounds. Economic instability, limited access to resources, and lower educational attainment are contributing factors.

Demographics

Understanding the demographics of teenage pregnancy is essential for developing targeted interventions:

- Geographic Distribution: Teenage pregnancy rates can vary significantly by region. Rural areas and certain urban neighborhoods may experience higher rates compared to suburban areas.

- **Educational Attainment:** Teenagers with lower levels of educational attainment are at a higher risk of early pregnancy. Education often plays a key role in shaping knowledge about sexual health and access to resources.
- **Family Dynamics:** Family structure and parental involvement can influence teenage pregnancy rates. Teens from single-parent households or those experiencing family instability may face increased risk.

Prevention Strategies

Effective prevention of teenage pregnancy requires a multifaceted approach that addresses education, access to resources, and supportive environments:

1. **Comprehensive Sex Education:** Providing comprehensive sex education that covers topics such as contraception, healthy relationships, and the consequences of early pregnancy is crucial. Programs should be age-appropriate and culturally sensitive.

2. **Access to Contraceptives:** Ensuring that teenagers have access to a range of contraceptive methods and information is vital. Schools, clinics, and community organizations can play a role in providing these resources.

3. **Parental Involvement:** Encouraging open communication between parents and teens about sexual health and relationships can help foster a supportive environment. Parents should be equipped with the knowledge and tools to discuss these topics effectively.

4. **Youth Empowerment:** Programs that empower young people with life skills, goal-setting, and self-esteem can reduce the likelihood of early pregnancy. Mentorship and leadership opportunities can also be beneficial.

5. **Community Support:** Communities can support teenage pregnancy prevention through initiatives that provide counseling, mentorship, and access to resources. Engaging local organizations and healthcare providers can enhance outreach efforts.

6. **Policy and Advocacy:** Advocating for policies that support comprehensive sex education, access to healthcare, and social support

services can create a more supportive environment for preventing teenage pregnancy.

Conclusion

Teenage pregnancy presents complex challenges that require coordinated efforts across various sectors. By understanding the statistics and demographics, and implementing effective prevention strategies, we can work towards reducing the rates of teenage pregnancy and supporting the well-being of young people.

Worksheet 1: Understanding Teenage Pregnancy Statistics and Demographics

Section 1: Analyzing Teenage Pregnancy Rates

1. **Data Interpretation:**
   - Based on the information provided in the chapter, what was the teen birth rate in the United States in 2023?
   - How does this rate compare to previous decades? What factors might have contributed to this change?

2. **Age Trends:**
   - Which age group has the highest rate of teenage pregnancies?
   - Why do you think teenage pregnancies are more common in this age group?

3. **Ethnic and Racial Disparities:**
   - Which ethnic groups have historically had higher rates of teenage pregnancy?
   - Discuss two possible reasons for these disparities. How might culturally tailored education and support programs help address these differences?

4. **Socioeconomic Factors:**
   - Explain how socioeconomic status can influence teenage pregnancy rates.
   - What are some challenges faced by teenagers from low-income backgrounds that may contribute to higher pregnancy rates?

5. **Geographic Distribution:**
   - How do teenage pregnancy rates differ between rural and urban areas?
   - Provide two reasons why certain regions might have higher teenage pregnancy rates.

Section 2: Reflection and Critical Thinking

6. **Educational Attainment and Pregnancy Risk:**
   - **Discuss the relationship between educational attainment and the risk of teenage pregnancy. Why is education important in shaping sexual health knowledge?**

7. **Family Dynamics:**
   - **How might family structure and parental involvement impact teenage pregnancy rates?**
   - **What role can parents play in reducing the risk of teenage pregnancy?**

Worksheet 2: Exploring Prevention Strategies for Teenage Pregnancy

Section 1: Prevention Strategy Analysis

1. **Comprehensive Sex Education:**
    - Define comprehensive sex education. What key topics should be included in such programs?
    - Why is it important for sex education to be age-appropriate and culturally sensitive?

2. **Access to Contraceptives:**
    - List three contraceptive methods that should be made available to teenagers.
    - How can schools and community organizations help ensure teenagers have access to these contraceptive methods?

3. **Parental Involvement:**
    - Discuss the importance of open communication between parents and teenagers about sexual health.
    - What are two ways parents can effectively discuss sexual health and relationships with their teens?

4. **Youth Empowerment:**
    - What life skills and self-esteem-building activities can help reduce the likelihood of teenage pregnancy?
    - How can mentorship and leadership opportunities empower young people and contribute to pregnancy prevention?

5. **Community Support:**
    - Explain the role of community organizations in supporting teenage pregnancy prevention.
    - What types of services or resources should these organizations provide to support teenagers?

6. **Policy and Advocacy:**
    - Why is it important to advocate for policies that support comprehensive sex education and access to healthcare?
    - Discuss one policy initiative that could help prevent teenage pregnancy.

Section 2: Personal Action Plan

7. **Creating a Prevention Plan:**
    - Based on what you've learned, create a brief action plan for preventing teenage pregnancy in your community. Consider the roles of education, access to resources, and community support.
    - How would you involve local schools, parents, and community organizations in your plan?

8. **Reflection:**
    - Reflect on the impact that preventing teenage pregnancy can have on individuals, families, and communities.
    - Why is it important to address teenage pregnancy not just as an individual issue, but as a societal challenge?

Chapter 7: Introduction to Assertiveness and the Importance of Saying No

Section 1: Start by asking students what they think "assertiveness" means. Discuss why it is important to be able to say "no" when necessary.

- Key Points to Cover:
  - Assertiveness when you have the ability to express what you think, how you feel, and what you need confidently, without being aggressive.
  - Saying "no" is crucial for maintaining personal boundaries and self-respect.
- Activity:
  - Have students think of a time when they wanted to say no but didn't. Ask them to share how they felt afterward.
  - Objective: Help students recognize the importance of standing firm in their decisions.

Section 2: Understanding Your Right to Say No

- Discuss that everyone has the right to refuse requests or invitations that make them uncomfortable or that they simply don't want to do.
- Example: If someone asks you to do something that goes against your values or makes you uncomfortable, you have every right to say no.2.2 Strategies for Saying No (15 minutes)

Section 3: Direct Approach:

- Example: "No, I can't commit to that right now."
- Activity: Practice with a partner. One student asks a favor, and the other uses the direct approach to decline.

Polite Approach:

- Example: "Thank you for thinking of me, but I have to decline."

- **Activity:** In pairs, role-play a scenario where the polite approach is used, such as declining an invitation.

Firm Approach:

- **Example:** "I am not available for this request. Please respect my decision."
- **Activity:** Students practice saying "no" firmly in a situation where they feel pressured. Discuss how it felt to be firm.

Section 4: Handling Guilt and Pressure

Discussion:

- Talk about common feelings after saying no, like guilt or anxiety. Explain that these feelings are natural but shouldn't dictate their actions.
- **Key Point:** Saying no is a form of self-care and should be respected.

- **Activity:**

    - **Group Sharing:** Students share their experiences of feeling guilty after saying no and brainstorm strategies to handle these emotions.
    - **Mindfulness Exercise:** Lead a brief mindfulness exercise to help students practice letting go of guilt and pressure.

Section 5: Understanding and Managing Peer Pressure (30 minutes)

Identifying Peer Pressure

Define peer pressure and discuss the different forms it can take (direct, indirect, subtle).

- **Direct:** Friends pressuring you to skip class.
- **Indirect:** Feeling the need to conform to what everyone else is doing at a party.
- **Subtle:** A friend making a comment that makes you feel bad for not joining in.

- Activity:

    Pressure to Cheat on a Test

    - **A classmate asks you directly to share your answers during a test.**
        - **Type: Direct**

Pressure to Skip Class

- **Scenario: Your friends skip class regularly and invite you to join them, saying things like, "Everyone's doing it."**
    - **Type: Indirect**

Pressure to Try Smoking

- **Scenario: A group of friends lights up a cigarette and casually offers you one, without saying anything more.**
    - **Type: Subtle**

Pressure to Change Your Appearance

- **Scenario: A friend makes a comment like, "You'd look so much cooler if you wore makeup like us."**
    - **Type: Subtle**

Pressure to Drink Alcohol

- **Scenario: At a party, someone hands you a drink and says, "Come on, just have one, it's no big deal."**
    - **Type: Direct**

Pressure to Join a Group Activity

- **Scenario: Your friends keep talking about how fun it is to play a certain sport, and they frequently suggest that you should join the team, even though you're not interested.**
    - **Type: Indirect**

Pressure to Engage in Gossip

- Scenario: A friend starts gossiping about another student and looks at you, expecting you to join in without explicitly asking you to.
    - Type: Subtle

Pressure to Lie to a Teacher

- Scenario: A friend asks you to cover for them by lying to a teacher about why they didn't do their homework, saying, "Just tell them I was sick."
    - Type: Direct

Pressure to Spend Money

- Scenario: Your friends frequently go out for expensive meals and shopping, and they keep inviting you, making you feel left out if you don't join.
    - Type: Indirect

Pressure to Post on Social Media

- Scenario: Your friends constantly post selfies and stories on social media and subtly comment on how you don't post as often, hinting that you should.
    - Type: Subtle

Section 6: Building a Support System

- Discussion:
    - Emphasize the importance of having supportive friends and mentors who respect their decisions and boundaries.
    - Key Points:
        - A strong support system helps reinforce positive decisions.
        - Friends who respect your "no" are true friends.
- Activity:
    - Create a Support Plan: Have students list people in their lives who they can rely on for support. Encourage them to think about how

these people can help them resist peer pressure. Also have students share ideas as a class on how to strengthen these support systems.

Closing Discussion: Share reflections and encourage students to practice these skills in their daily lives.

This lesson plan will help students build the confidence and skills needed to assert themselves, handle peer pressure, and maintain their personal boundaries.

Worksheet 1: Understanding and Practicing Assertiveness

Section 1: What is Assertiveness?

1. **Define Assertiveness:**
    - In your own words, what does "assertiveness" mean?
    - Why is it important to express what you think, feel, and need confidently?

2. **Reflection:**
    - Think of a time when you wanted to say "no" but didn't. How did you feel afterward? Write a brief description of the situation and your feelings.

3. **Discussion Prompt:**
    - Share your experience with a partner or in a small group. Discuss why it can be difficult to say "no" and why it's important to stand firm in your decisions.

Section 2: Your Right to Say No

4. **Understanding Your Rights:**
    - Why do you have the right to say "no" to requests or invitations that make you uncomfortable?
    - Write down an example of a situation where you might need to say "no" to protect your personal boundaries.

5. **Discussion:**
    - Discuss with a partner or group how saying "no" in these situations could benefit your well-being.

Section 3: Strategies for Saying No

6. **Practice Saying No:**

    o **Direct Approach:** Write your own version of a direct response to this scenario: A friend asks you to help them with a project that you don't have time for.

    - Example: "No, I can't commit to that right now."
    - Your Response: _____

    o **Polite Approach:** Write a polite response to this scenario: You're invited to a party, but you don't want to go.

    - Example: "Thank you for thinking of me, but I have to decline."
    - Your Response: _____

    o **Firm Approach:** Write a firm response to this scenario: You feel pressured to do something against your values.

    - Example: "I am not available for this request. Please respect my decision."
    - Your Response: _____

7. **Role-Playing Activity:**

    o **Pair up with a partner and practice each approach by taking turns asking each other for favors and using the different strategies to say "no."**

Worksheet 2: Handling Peer Pressure and Building a Support System

Section 4: Identifying and Managing Peer Pressure

1. **Identifying Peer Pressure:**
   - Match the following scenarios to the type of peer pressure they represent (Direct, Indirect, Subtle):
     - A classmate asks you directly to share your answers during a test. (Type: _____)
     - Your friends skip class regularly and invite you to join them, saying things like, "Everyone's doing it." (Type: _____)
     - A friend makes a comment like, "You'd look so much cooler if you wore makeup like us." (Type: _____)

2. **Reflection:**
   - Have you ever experienced peer pressure? Describe a situation where you felt pressured to do something you weren't comfortable with. How did you handle it?

3. **Discussion Prompt:**
   - Share your experiences in a small group. Discuss how you felt during the situation and what you could do differently next time.

Section 5: Building a Support System

4. **Support Plan:**
    - List three people in your life who you can rely on for support when facing peer pressure. How can each of these people help you resist pressure?
        - Person 1: _____
            1. (Support: _____)
        - Person 2: _____
            1. (Support: _____)
        - Person 3: _____
            1. (Support: _____)

5. **Class Activity:**
    - Share ideas as a class on how to strengthen support systems. What are some ways you can help each other maintain boundaries and say "no" confidently?

Section 6: Coping with Guilt and Pressure

6. **Mindfulness Exercise:**
    - Practice a brief mindfulness exercise to help let go of guilt and pressure. Write down how you felt before and after the exercise.

7. **Reflection:**
    - Why is it important to recognize and manage feelings of guilt after saying "no"? How can this help you maintain your personal boundaries?

Chapter 8: Effective Communication

To equip learners with the skills needed for effective verbal and non-verbal communication, enhance their ability to actively listen and empathize, and resolve conflicts through respectful communication.

Section 1: Tips for Effective Verbal and Non-Verbal Communication

Clear and Concise Expression:

- Use simple, direct language to convey your message.
- Avoid jargon and complex terminology unless necessary.
- Structure your message logically with a clear beginning, middle, and end.

Tone and Pitch:

- Maintain a tone that is calm and respectful.
- Be mindful of your pitch to avoid sounding aggressive or disinterested.

Volume and Pace:

- Speak at an appropriate volume for the setting, ensuring you are heard without shouting.
- Adjust your speaking pace to allow for understanding and engagement.

Feedback and Clarification:

- Encourage questions and provide feedback to ensure mutual understanding.
- Clarify any points of confusion immediately to avoid miscommunication.

Non-Verbal Communication

Body Language:

- Maintain open and relaxed posture to convey openness and receptivity.
- Use appropriate gestures to emphasize points, but avoid excessive movements.

Eye Contact:

- Establish and maintain eye contact to show engagement and sincerity.
- Avoid staring, which can be intimidating, and ensure it is culturally appropriate.

Facial Expressions:

- Use facial expressions that match your verbal message to reinforce your words.
- Be aware of your expressions to avoid sending mixed signals.

Personal Space:

- Respect personal space boundaries to avoid discomfort.
- Adjust your proximity based on the context and relationship with the other person.

Section 2: Importance of Active Listening and Empathy

Active Listening

Paying Full Attention:

- Focus entirely on the speaker without distractions.
- Use non-verbal cues, such as nodding, to show attentiveness.

Reflecting and Paraphrasing:

- Repeat back or paraphrase what the speaker has said to confirm understanding.
- Reflect on their emotions to show that you understand their perspective.

Avoiding Interruptions:

- Let the speaker finish their thoughts before responding.
- Allow pauses in conversation to give space for further elaboration.

Asking Clarifying Questions:

- Use open-ended questions to gain deeper insights and ensure clear understanding.

- Avoid leading or judgmental questions that could bias the response.

Empathy

Understanding Emotions:

- Recognize and validate the speaker's emotions, even if you don't agree with their perspective.
- Use empathetic statements like "I can see why you feel that way" or "That sounds really challenging."

Demonstrating Compassion:

- Offer support and understanding, acknowledging the speaker's experience.
- Show genuine concern and willingness to help where possible.

Avoiding Judgment:

- Keep an open mind and avoid making assumptions about the speaker's feelings or experiences.
- Focus on understanding their point of view rather than critiquing it.

Section 3: Resolving Conflicts Through Communication

Identifying the Issue

Clear Definition:

- Clearly identify the root cause of the conflict.
- Ensure that all parties involved have a shared understanding of the issue.

Acknowledging Perspectives:

- Recognize and validate each party's perspective on the conflict.
- Avoid dismissing or minimizing others' viewpoints.

Constructive Dialogue

Using "I" Statements:

- **Express your feelings and concerns using "I" statements to avoid placing blame (e.g., "I feel frustrated when…").**
- **Focus on your own experiences rather than criticizing others.**

Finding Common Ground:

- **Look for areas of agreement and build on them to find mutually acceptable solutions.**
- **Emphasize shared goals and interests to foster collaboration.**

Negotiation and Compromise:

- **Be open to negotiating and finding a middle ground that respects everyone's needs and interests.**
- **Approach compromise with flexibility and a willingness to adapt.**

Conclusion:

Effective communication is vital for building strong relationships and resolving conflicts. By practicing clear and respectful verbal and non-verbal communication, actively listening, and empathizing with others, you can foster a positive and productive environment. Mastering these skills will not only improve your interactions but also contribute to personal and professional growth.

Worksheet 1: Understanding Verbal and Non-Verbal Communication

Section 1: Tips for Effective Verbal Communication

A. Matching Exercise: Match the communication tips with their correct descriptions.

1. Clear and Concise Expression
   a) Speak at an appropriate volume for the setting.

2. Tone and Pitch
   b) Encourage questions and provide feedback to ensure mutual understanding.

3. Volume and Pace
   c) Maintain a calm and respectful tone.

4. Feedback and Clarification
   d) Use simple, direct language and avoid jargon.

B. Practice Activity: Imagine you are giving instructions to a group of new students on how to navigate the school. Write a short paragraph using clear and concise language. Pay attention to your tone and how you would adjust your volume and pace.

Section 2: Non-Verbal Communication

A. True or False: Write "True" or "False" next to each statement.

1. ___ Maintaining eye contact is a sign of engagement and sincerity.

2. ___ Excessive gestures are recommended to emphasize points during communication.

3. ___ Personal space boundaries should be ignored if you want to show enthusiasm.

4. ___ Facial expressions should match the verbal message to avoid sending mixed signals.

B. Role-Playing: In pairs, practice a conversation where you focus on using effective non-verbal communication. One person should speak while the other responds with appropriate body language, eye contact, and facial expressions. Switch roles after a few minutes.

Worksheet 2: Active Listening, Empathy, and Conflict Resolution

Section 1: Importance of Active Listening and Empathy

A. Multiple Choice: Choose the correct answer for each question.

1. What is the best way to show that you are actively listening?

    a) Interrupting the speaker
    b) Looking away frequently
    c) Nodding and using non-verbal cues
    d) Responding before the speaker finishes

2. Which of the following is an example of empathetic communication?

    a) "I can see why you feel that way."
    b) "You should get over it."
    c) "It's not that big of a deal."
    d) "Why do you always feel that way?"

3. What should you avoid doing when trying to understand someone's emotions?

    a) Recognizing their emotions
    b) Making assumptions about their feelings
    c) Offering support
    d) Listening carefully

B. Reflection: Think about a time when someone didn't listen to you effectively. How did it make you feel? Write a short paragraph about the experience and what could have been done differently.

Section 2: Resolving Conflicts Through Communication

A. Fill in the Blanks: Complete the sentences using the following words: "I", compromise, perspectives, issue.

1. Use ___ statements to express your feelings without placing blame.
2. The first step in resolving a conflict is to clearly define the ___.
3. A successful conflict resolution often involves finding a ___.
4. It is important to acknowledge all parties' ___ during a conflict.

B. Conflict Resolution Role-Play: In pairs, choose a conflict scenario (e.g., disagreement over group project roles). Use the following steps to resolve the conflict:

1. Identify the issue.
2. Acknowledge each other's perspectives.
3. Use "I" statements to express feelings.
4. Find common ground.
5. Negotiate a compromise.

After the role-play, discuss how effective the communication was and what could have been improved.

Chapter 9: Furthering Your Education

Why Education Matters

Objective:

To highlight the importance of education, explore various educational paths, and guide learners in setting and achieving their educational goals.

Section 1: Benefits of Higher Education and Vocational Training

Personal Growth and Development

Knowledge and Skills Acquisition:

- Gain advanced knowledge in specialized fields.
- Develop practical skills relevant to career and personal interests.

Critical Thinking and Problem-Solving:

- Enhance analytical abilities and problem-solving skills.
- Cultivate critical thinking through coursework and hands-on experiences.

Confidence and Self-Efficacy:

- Build confidence in one's abilities through academic achievements.
- Develop a sense of self-efficacy and independence.

Career Advancement

Improved Job Prospects:

- Increase employability and access to a wider range of job opportunities.
- Higher educational qualifications often lead to higher starting salaries and career growth.

Skill Specialization:

- Gain expertise in a specific area, making you more competitive in the job market.
- Obtain certifications or qualifications that are valued by employers.

Professional Networking:

- Build a network of professional contacts through educational institutions and programs.
- Leverage connections for career opportunities and mentorship.

Economic and Social Benefits

Economic Stability:

- Higher levels of education are linked to higher income potential and financial stability.
- Access to better job security and benefits.

Social Impact:

- Contribute positively to society through enhanced skills and knowledge.
- Engage in community service and leadership roles.

Lifelong Learning:

- Cultivate a habit of lifelong learning and adaptability.
- Stay current with industry trends and technological advancements.

Section 2: Exploring Different Educational Paths

Higher Education

Traditional College and University Degrees:

- Understand the structure of undergraduate, graduate, and doctoral programs.
- Explore fields of study, such as liberal arts, sciences, engineering, and business.

Professional Degrees and Certifications:

- Learn about specialized programs for careers in law, medicine, education, and more.
- Understand the importance of licensure and certification for certain professions.

Online and Distance Learning:

- Explore the benefits and flexibility of online courses and degree programs.
- Understand how to balance online learning with other responsibilities.

Vocational and Technical Training

Trade Schools and Technical Colleges:

- Learn about programs that provide hands-on training in fields like plumbing, electrical work, and automotive repair.
- Understand the value of certifications and apprenticeships.

Short-Term Courses and Bootcamps:

- Explore options for short-term training programs in areas such as coding, design, and business skills.
- Understand how these programs can quickly enhance your skillset.

Industry Certifications:

- Learn about certifications that validate expertise in specific tools, technologies, or methodologies.
- Understand how certifications can improve job prospects and career advancement.

Alternative Education Paths

Self-Directed Learning:

- Explore ways to learn independently through resources like books, online courses, and workshops.
- Understand the benefits of self-directed learning for personal and professional development.

Community Education and Workshops:

- Learn about local community education programs and workshops.
- Explore opportunities for skill-building and personal enrichment.

Experiential Learning:

- **Understand the value of hands-on experiences, internships, and volunteer work.**
- **Explore how experiential learning complements formal education.**

Section 3: Setting Educational Goals

Identifying Your Objectives

Self-Assessment:

- **Evaluate your interests, strengths, and career aspirations.**
- **Reflect on how education aligns with your personal and professional goals.**

Research and Exploration:

- **Investigate different educational programs and paths that align with your objectives.**
- **Consider factors such as program content, duration, cost, and career outcomes.**

Goal Setting

SMART Goals: LOOK BACK AT CHAPTER 3

Short-Term vs. Long-Term Goals:

- **Differentiate between short-term goals (e.g., completing a course) and long-term goals (e.g., earning a degree).**
- **Develop a plan to achieve both types of goals.**

Creating an Action Plan:

- **Outline the steps needed to achieve your educational goals, including research, application, and enrollment processes.**
- **Set deadlines and milestones to track your progress.**

Overcoming Challenges

Managing Time and Resources:

- **Develop strategies for balancing education with other responsibilities.**

- Explore financial aid, scholarships, and budgeting for educational expenses.

Staying Motivated:

- Identify sources of motivation and support to keep you focused on your goals.
- Create a support network of peers, mentors, and advisors.

Adapting to Change:

- Be prepared to adjust your goals and plans as needed.
- Embrace flexibility and resilience in the face of challenges.

Conclusion:

Education plays a crucial role in personal and professional development. By understanding the benefits of higher education and vocational training, exploring various educational paths, and setting clear goals, you can make informed decisions about your educational journey and achieve your aspirations.

Worksheet 1: Understanding the Benefits of Education

Objective: Identify and reflect on the personal, career, and social benefits of furthering your education.

Instructions: Read through the benefits of higher education and vocational training in Section 1 of Chapter 9. Then, answer the following questions.

Part 1: Personal Growth and Development

1. Knowledge and Skills Acquisition

    - What are three areas in which you would like to gain advanced knowledge or develop practical skills? Explain why these are important to you.
        - a.
        - b.
        - c.

2. Critical Thinking and Problem-Solving

    - Describe a situation where you had to use critical thinking or problem-solving skills. How do you think further education could enhance these skills?

3. Confidence and Self-Efficacy

    - Reflect on a time when you felt confident in your abilities. How did education or learning contribute to that confidence?

Part 2: Career Advancement

1. Improved Job Prospects

    - List three careers or jobs you are interested in. What level of education or training is typically required for each?
        - a.
        - b.
        - c.

2. Skill Specialization
    - What specific skills do you want to specialize in? How could vocational training or higher education help you develop these skills?

3. Professional Networking
    - Why is professional networking important? How do you plan to build and maintain your network through your educational journey?

Part 3: Economic and Social Benefits

1. Economic Stability
    - How do you think higher education or vocational training could contribute to your financial stability in the future?

2. Social Impact
    - In what ways do you hope to contribute to society through your education? List at least two potential impacts you want to make.

3. Lifelong Learning
    - Why is it important to cultivate a habit of lifelong learning? How do you plan to stay current with industry trends and advancements?

Worksheet 2: Exploring Educational Paths and Setting Goals

Objective: Explore different educational paths and create a plan for setting and achieving your educational goals.

Instructions: Use the information from Section 2 and Section 3 of Chapter 9 to answer the following questions.

Part 1: Exploring Educational Paths

1. Higher Education

    - Research one traditional college or university degree program you are interested in. What are the key components of this program? How does it align with your career goals?

2. Vocational and Technical Training

    - Identify a vocational or technical training program that interests you. What skills will you learn in this program? How will these skills make you more competitive in the job market?

3. Alternative Education Paths

    - What is one alternative education path (e.g., self-directed learning, community education, experiential learning) that appeals to you? How could it complement your formal education?

Part 2: Setting Educational Goals

1. Identifying Your Objectives

    - What are your main educational objectives? Reflect on your interests, strengths, and career aspirations. Write down at least three objectives.

        - a.
        - b.
        - c.

2. **Research and Exploration**
    - **Investigate one educational program that aligns with your objectives. What are the program content, duration, cost, and potential career outcomes?**

3. **Goal Setting**
    - **Using the SMART goals framework (from Chapter 3), create one short-term and one long-term educational goal. Write down your goals and the specific steps you will take to achieve them.**
        - Short-term Goal:
        - Steps:
        - Long-term Goal:
        - Steps:

4. **Overcoming Challenges**
    - **What challenges might you face in achieving your educational goals? How will you manage your time, resources, and motivation to overcome these challenges?**

Conclusion: After completing these worksheets, reflect on how your education can shape your future. What steps will you take next to further your education and achieve your goals? Write a short paragraph summarizing your action plan.

Chapter 10: Great Hygiene Practices

Introduction to Personal Hygiene

- What is personal hygiene? Personal hygiene is when individuals maintain cleanliness and health. This includes routine activities like bathing, brushing teeth, and washing hands, which help prevent the spread of germs and maintain a healthy body.

Overview of Personal Hygiene Practices

Personal hygiene practices involve daily routines that contribute to overall well-being. These routines help protect the body from infections, diseases, and unpleasant odors, while also enhancing self-esteem and social interactions.

The Role of Personal Hygiene in Health and Well-Being

- How personal hygiene contributes to overall health: Personal hygiene is essential for preventing illnesses caused by bacteria, viruses, and fungi. By maintaining good hygiene, you reduce the risk of infections, improve skin health, and enhance your body's overall function.

- The connection between hygiene and quality of life: Good hygiene practices contribute to a higher quality of life by improving physical health, boosting confidence, and positively impacting social interactions.

1. Daily Hygiene Routines and Their Importance

Morning Routine

- Brushing teeth: Techniques and frequency: Brush your teeth twice a day (morning and night) for at least two minutes each time.

- Washing the face: Benefits for skin health: Wash your face every morning to remove oil, dirt, and dead skin cells. This helps prevent acne, refreshes your skin, and prepares it for the day.

- Showering or bathing: Importance and frequency: Shower or bathe daily to remove sweat, dirt, and bacteria from your skin. Regular bathing keeps your skin clean, prevents body odor, and promotes a sense of well-being.

Throughout the Day

- **Hand washing: When and how to wash hands properly:** Wash your hands with soap and water:
    - Before eating or preparing food
    - After using the restroom
    - After touching garbage or dirty surfaces
    - After coughing, sneezing, or blowing your nose
    - Before and after caring for someone who is sick
- **Proper handwashing involves scrubbing all parts of your hands, including the backs, between fingers, and under nails, for at least 20 seconds.**
- **Managing sweat and body odor: Use of deodorants and antiperspirants:** Apply deodorant or antiperspirant daily, especially after showering. Deodorants mask body odor, while antiperspirants reduce sweat production, helping you stay fresh throughout the day.
- **Staying hydrated and its effect on skin and overall health:** Drinking eight glasses of water a day is sufficient. Staying hydrated helps maintain skin elasticity, prevents dryness, and supports overall bodily functions, including digestion and circulation.

Evening Routine

- **Cleansing skin before bed: Importance of removing makeup and impurities:** Cleanse your face before bed to remove makeup, dirt, and oil accumulated throughout the day. This prevents clogged pores, reduces the risk of acne, and allows your skin to repair overnight.
- **Dental care: Brushing and flossing before sleep:** Floss and brush your teeth before you go to bed. This helps prevent cavities, gum disease, and bad breath.
- **Preparing for a good night's sleep:** Importance of a clean and comfortable environment that is free from distractions. Regularly change your bed linens, keep your bedroom at a comfortable temperature, and create a calming bedtime routine to promote restful sleep.

1. **Impact of Hygiene on Health and Confidence**

Health Benefits of Good Hygiene

- **Preventing infections and illnesses:** Good hygiene practices, such as handwashing and regular bathing, help prevent spreading infectious diseases like a colds, or the flu, and skin infections.

- **Reducing the spread of germs and bacteria:** Regularly washing hands, cleaning surfaces, and maintaining personal cleanliness helps to reduce of harmful bacteria being spread around and viruses, protecting both yourself and others.

- **Maintaining a healthy skin and body:** Regular skin care and hygiene practices prevent issues like acne, rashes, and infections, keeping your skin and body healthy and vibrant.

Psychological Impact of Hygiene

- **How personal hygiene affects self-esteem and confidence:** Good hygiene boosts self-esteem by making you feel clean, fresh, and presentable. It also reduces anxiety about body odor or appearance, enhancing confidence in social situations.

- **The role of cleanliness in social interactions and self-perception:** Cleanliness positively impacts how others perceive you and how you perceive yourself. It promotes positive social interactions, fosters respect, and contributes to a strong sense of self-worth.

Cultural and Social Considerations

- **Understanding different hygiene practices across cultures:** Hygiene practices vary across cultures based on traditions, climate, and available resources. Understanding and respecting these differences is important in fostering cultural sensitivity and inclusivity.

- **Respecting personal and social hygiene norms:** Be mindful of personal and social hygiene norms, especially when interacting with people from different backgrounds. Respect others' practices and preferences while maintaining your own hygiene standards.

1. **Specific Hygiene Practices for Boys and Girls**

Hygiene Practices for Boys

- **Hair care: Shampooing, conditioning, and grooming:** Shampoo your hair 2-3 times a week to remove dirt and excess oil. Use conditioner to keep hair soft and manageable. Regularly groom your hair to maintain a neat appearance.

- **Avoid touching your face with dirty hands to prevent breakouts.**

- **Personal grooming: Shaving and trimming:** Shave or trim facial hair as needed to maintain a clean or well-groomed appearance. Use a sharp razor, shaving cream, and aftershave to prevent irritation.

- **Specific concerns: Dealing with body odor and sweating:** Shower daily, especially after physical activity. Use deodorant or antiperspirant to manage body odor and sweat. Wear clean clothes and change them regularly.

Hygiene Practices for Girls

- Hair care: Shampooing, conditioning, and styling: Shampoo your hair 2-3 times a week, and use conditioner to keep it soft and healthy. Style your hair in a way that suits your preferences, ensuring it is neat and clean.

- Skin care: Managing acne and maintaining skin health: Cleanse, tone, and moisturize your skin daily. Use products suited to your skin type to manage acne and maintain a healthy complexion. Avoid heavy makeup that can clog pores.

- Personal grooming: Hair removal and personal care: Hair removal is a personal choice. If you choose to remove body hair, use methods like shaving, waxing, or depilatory creams. Always follow proper techniques to avoid irritation.

- Menstrual hygiene: Managing menstrual cycles and products: During menstruation, change sanitary products (pads, tampons, menstrual cups) regularly to prevent infections and maintain comfort. Wash your genital area with a mild soap and water to help you with your good hygiene.

This lesson gives an easy overview of personal hygiene practices, tailored to address the needs and concerns of both boys and girls. Students should be encouraged to ask questions and share their thoughts to ensure they understand how important it is to maintain good hygiene daily.

Worksheet 1: Personal Hygiene Knowledge Check

Answer the following questions based on what you've learned in Chapter 10.

1. Define personal hygiene and explain why it is important.

_____

_____

2. List three daily hygiene routines and describe their importance.

a. Routine:

_____

Importance:

_____

b. Routine:

_____

Importance:

_____

c. Routine:

_____

Importance:

_____

3. How does maintaining good hygiene contribute to overall health and well-being?

_____

_____

4. Explain the benefits of staying hydrated for personal hygiene.

_____

_____

5. Describe how personal hygiene can impact self-esteem and social interactions.

_____

6. What are some cultural considerations when it comes to hygiene practices?

_____

_____

7. For boys and girls, list two specific hygiene practices and explain their importance.

a. Boys:
_____

Importance:
_____

b. Girls:
_____

Importance:
_____

Bonus Question: How can understanding and respecting different hygiene practices help in building a more inclusive environment?

_____

_____

Worksheet 2: Create Your Own Hygiene Routine

Use the space below to design your personal hygiene routine based on what you've learned. Be sure to include both morning and evening routines, as well as any practices throughout the day.

Morning Routine:

1. **Brushing Teeth:**
    - **How often?**
    _____
    - **Techniques:**
    _____

2. **Washing Face:**
    - **How often?**
    _____
    - **Benefits:**
    _____

3. **Showering/Bathing:**
    - **Frequency:**
    _____
    - **Importance:**
    _____

Throughout the Day:

1. **Hand Washing:**
    - **When to wash:**
    _____
    - **How to wash:**
    _____

2. **Managing Sweat and Body Odor:**
    - Products used:
      _____
    - Frequency of use:
      _____

3. **Hydration:**
    - Amount of water per day:
      _____
    - Effect on health:
      _____

Evening Routine:

1. **Cleansing Skin:**
    - How to clean:
      _____
    - Importance:
      _____

2. **Dental Care:**
    - Brushing and flossing:
      _____
    - Frequency:
      _____

3. **Preparing for Sleep:**
    - Bed linens:
      _____
    - Room environment:
      _____
    - How does your routine make you feel?
      _____

Chapter 11: Stop Bullying

Recognizing and Responding to Bullying

Objective: To understand different types of bullying, their effects, and to develop effective strategies for dealing with bullies, while emphasizing the importance of empathy and support for victims.

Section 1: Introduction to Bullying

- Bullying is intentional, aggressive behavior that involves an imbalance of power or strength. It can be physical, verbal, or social, and is typically repeated over time. Bullying can also be threatening people, purposely not allowing someone to be a part of a group, and spreading rumors. The goal of bullying is often to harm, control, or humiliate the target, leading to significant emotional, psychological, or physical distress.

Section 2: Types of Bullying and Their Effects

Objective: Identify different types of bullying and understand their effects on victims.

1. Types of Bullying:
    - **Physical Bullying:** Hitting, kicking, pushing.
    - **Verbal Bullying:** Name-calling, threats, teasing.
    - **Social Bullying:** Exclusion, spreading rumors, manipulating social relationships.
    - **Cyberbullying:** Harassment through digital platforms (social media, texting).

2. Effects of Bullying:
    - Short-term effects: Anxiety, depression, physical injuries.
    - Long-term effects: Low self-esteem, academic problems, chronic mental health issues.

Section 3: Strategies for Dealing with Bullies

Objective: Develop and practice effective strategies for addressing and preventing bullying.

1. **For Victims:**
   - **Assertiveness Training:** How to stand up for oneself without aggression.
   - **Seeking Help:** When and how to approach trusted adults or authorities.

2. **For Bystanders:**
   - **Intervening Safely:** How to safely intervene or report bullying.
   - **Supporting the Victim:** Ways to provide emotional support and encouragement.

3. **For Educators and Parents:**
   - **Creating a Safe Environment:** Implementing anti-bullying policies and fostering a positive atmosphere.
   - **Engagement with Students:** Regular discussions and education about bullying prevention.

Section 4: Importance of Empathy and Support for Victims

1. **Understanding Empathy:**
   - Definition and importance of empathy.
   - How empathy can help in preventing and addressing bullying.

2. **Providing Support:**
   - Practical ways to offer support to victims (listening, encouraging, helping them find resources).
   - Importance of a supportive network for recovery and resilience.

This curriculum can be adapted for different age groups and settings. The key is to create an engaging and interactive learning experience that empowers participants to recognize, address, and prevent bullying effectively.

Worksheet 1: Understanding and Identifying Bullying

Answer the following questions based on what you've learned in Chapter 11.

1. Define bullying and list three different types of bullying.

Definition:
_____

Types of Bullying:

a.
_____

b.
_____

c.
_____

d.
_____

2. Match the type of bullying with its example:

a. Physical Bullying
b. Verbal Bullying
c. Social Bullying
d. Cyberbullying

Examples:

1. Sending hurtful messages online or through text.
2. Excluding someone from a group activity.
3. Calling someone names or making threats.
4. Hitting or pushing someone.

Matching:

a. _____
b. _____
c. _____
d. _____

3. **List two short-term and two long-term effects of bullying.**

Short-term Effects:

a.
_____

b.
_____

Long-term Effects:

a.
_____

b.
_____

4. **Explain why it is important to address bullying and the impact it can have on a victim's life.**

_____

_____

5. **Identify one real-life situation where bullying could occur and describe which type of bullying it might be.**

Situation:
_____

Type of Bullying:
_____

Worksheet 2: Strategies for Dealing with Bullies and Supporting Victims

Use the space below to think about and write down effective strategies for dealing with bullies and supporting victims, based on what you've learned in Chapter 11.

For Victims:

1. Assertiveness Training:
    - Describe how a victim can stand up for themselves without being aggressive.

_____
_____

2. Seeking Help:
    - When should a victim approach trusted adults or authorities, and how can they do so?

_____
_____

For Bystanders:

1. Intervening Safely:
    - How can bystanders safely intervene or report bullying?

_____
_____

2. Supporting the Victim:
   - List ways to provide emotional support and encouragement to a victim.

___

___

For Educators and Parents:

1. Creating a Safe Environment:
   - What can educators and parents do to create a safe environment and implement anti-bullying policies?

___

2. Engagement with Students:
   - How can educators and parents engage with students to prevent bullying?

___

Understanding Empathy:

1. Definition and Importance of Empathy:
   - Define empathy and explain why it is important in preventing and addressing bullying.

___

___

2. **Providing Support:**
    - **List practical ways to offer support to victims and why a supportive network is crucial for recovery.**

_____

_____

Reflection:

- **How can understanding and practicing empathy help reduce bullying in schools or communities?**

_____

_____

Chapter 12: Chores and Cleanliness

Importance of a Clean Environment

Objective:

Understand the responsibilities and benefits of doing chores, learn practical tips for maintaining a clean living space, and recognize the importance of cleanliness in both personal and shared spaces.

Section 1: Introduction to Chores and Cleanliness

Define chores and cleanliness, and explain their significance in maintaining a healthy and organized environment.

- **Definition of Chores:** Chores are regular tasks or duties that individuals perform to help maintain the cleanliness, order, and functionality of a living environment. These tasks can vary in frequency and difficulty, ranging from daily to seasonal activities.

- **Definition of Cleanliness:** Cleanliness refers to the practice of keeping oneself, one's belongings, and one's surroundings clean and free from dirt, germs, and clutter. It involves routine cleaning, organizing, and maintaining hygiene in both personal and shared spaces.

- **Significance of Chores and Cleanliness:** Maintaining cleanliness through regular chores is essential for a healthy, safe, and pleasant living environment. Cleanliness helps prevent the spread of germs, reduces stress, and creates a space where everyone feels comfortable and respected.

Section 2. Responsibilities and Benefits of Doing Chores

Objective:

Identify the responsibilities associated with chores and understand their benefits.

Content:

1. **Types of Chores:**
   - **Daily Chores:**
     - **Making the bed:** Ensures a neat and organized start to the day.
     - **Washing dishes:** Prevents the buildup of dirty dishes and keeps the kitchen clean.
     - **Tidying up:** Regularly putting away items and keeping surfaces clear helps maintain order.
   - **Weekly Chores:**
     - **Vacuuming:** Removes dust, dirt, and allergens from floors and carpets.
     - **Dusting:** Prevents the buildup of dust on surfaces, which can trigger allergies.
     - **Cleaning bathrooms:** Ensures hygiene by removing soap scum, mold, and germs.
   - **Monthly/Seasonal Chores:**
     - **Deep cleaning:** Involves thorough cleaning of areas not addressed in daily or weekly chores, such as behind furniture or under appliances.
     - **Organizing closets:** Keeps clothing and personal items sorted and accessible.
     - **Yard work:** Maintains the exterior of the home, including mowing the lawn, raking leaves, and gardening.
2. **Benefits of Doing Chores:**
   - **Personal Benefits:**
     - **Develops responsibility:** Completing chores teaches accountability and self-discipline.

- Improves time management: Learning to balance chores with other activities helps develop time management skills.
- Builds life skills: Chores teach essential life skills, such as cleaning, organizing, and maintaining a home.

- Family Benefits:
  - Contributes to a harmonious household: When everyone contributes, the home runs more smoothly and feels more balanced.
  - Teaches teamwork and cooperation: Sharing chores fosters collaboration and helps family members learn to work together.

- Health Benefits:
  - Reduces allergens: Regular cleaning removes dust, pet dander, and other allergens that can affect health.
  - Prevents the spread of germs: Cleaning and disinfecting surfaces help reduce the risk of illness.
  - Promotes mental well-being: A clean and organized environment can reduce stress and improve focus.

- Impact of Assigning Chores on Household Dynamics:
  - Assigning chores helps distribute responsibilities evenly, preventing resentment and ensuring that everyone contributes to the upkeep of the home. It also fosters a sense of teamwork and accountability within the household.

Section 3: Tips for Maintaining a Clean Living Space

Objective:

Learn practical tips and strategies for keeping living spaces clean and organized.

Content:

1. **Daily Cleaning Habits:**
   - **Declutter:**
     - Regularly clear surfaces of unnecessary items. A clutter-free space is easier to clean and maintain, reducing stress and making the environment more pleasant.
   - **Spot Cleaning:**
     - Address spills, stains, and messes immediately to prevent them from becoming harder to clean later. This helps maintain the overall cleanliness of the space.
   - **Regular Maintenance:**
     - Stick to a daily cleaning routine, such as wiping down surfaces, sweeping floors, and putting away items. Consistency prevents dirt and clutter from accumulating.

2. **Weekly Cleaning Routines:**
   - **Deep Cleaning Tasks:**
     - Set aside time each week for more intensive cleaning tasks, like vacuuming, dusting, and mopping floors. This keeps your living space hygienic and fresh.
   - **Sanitizing:**
     - Regularly clean and disinfect high-touch areas such as doorknobs, light switches, and remote controls to reduce the spread of germs.

3. **Organizational Tips:**
   - **Storage Solutions:**
     - Use bins, shelves, and organizers to keep belongings in order. Proper storage helps maintain a tidy space and makes it easier to find items when needed.

- Labeling:
    - Label storage containers and shelves to ensure everything has a designated place. This makes organization more efficient and helps everyone know where things belong.

Section 4: Importance of Cleanliness in Personal and Shared Spaces

Objective:

Understand the significance of maintaining cleanliness in both personal and shared spaces and its impact on everyone involved.

Content:

1. Personal Spaces:
    - Self-Care:
        - Personal cleanliness, including maintaining a tidy bedroom and personal belongings, contributes to physical and mental well-being. A clean environment can improve mood, enhance focus, and promote a sense of pride in one's living area.
    - Pride and Responsibility:
        - Taking ownership of one's personal space fosters a sense of responsibility and self-respect. It encourages good habits that can extend to other areas of life.
2. Shared Spaces:
    - Respect and Consideration:
        - Keeping common areas tidy shows respect for others who share the space. It helps create a comfortable and welcoming environment for everyone.
    - Conflict Prevention:
        - A clean and organized shared space reduces the likelihood of conflicts over messiness or responsibilities. It promotes harmony and positive interactions among those living or working together.

This lesson plan provides a thorough understanding of the importance of chores and cleanliness, offering students the knowledge and practical tips needed to maintain a clean and organized living space. Encourage students to reflect on how these practices can improve their daily lives and contribute to a positive home environment.

Worksheet 1: Understanding Chores and Cleanliness

Answer the following questions based on what you've learned in Chapter 12.

1. Define the following terms:

    o **Chores:**
    _____

    o **Cleanliness:**
    _____

2. List and describe three types of chores and their importance.

a. Daily Chores:

    o Type:
    _____

    o Description and Importance:
    _____

b. Weekly Chores:

    o Type:
    _____

    o Description and Importance:
    _____

c. Monthly/Seasonal Chores:

    o Type:
    _____

    o Description and Importance:
    _____

3. Explain two personal benefits and two family benefits of doing chores.

Personal Benefits:

a.
_____

b.
_____

Family Benefits:

a.
_____

b.
_____

4. **Describe two health benefits of maintaining cleanliness in your living space.**

a.
_____

b.
_____

5. **Why is it important to distribute chores evenly in a household?**

_____

_____

6. **Provide an example of a chore you are responsible for and explain how it contributes to a clean and organized environment.**

Chore:
_____

Contribution to Cleanliness:
_____

_____

Worksheet 2: Tips for Maintaining a Clean Living Space

Complete the exercises and questions below to learn and apply practical tips for keeping your living space clean and organized.

1. Daily Cleaning Habits:

a. Declutter:

- Describe how decluttering can make cleaning easier and more efficient.

_____

_____

b. Spot Cleaning:

- Explain why it's important to address spills and messes immediately.

_____

_____

c. Regular Maintenance:

- List three daily tasks you can include in your cleaning routine.

    1. _____
    2. _____
    3. _____

2. **Importance of Cleanliness in Personal and Shared Spaces:**

a. **Personal Spaces:**
- Describe how maintaining cleanliness in your personal space can affect your well-being.

_____
_____

b. **Shared Spaces:**
- Explain why it is important to keep shared spaces clean and how it prevents conflicts.

_____
_____

3. **Reflection:**
- Think about a time when maintaining cleanliness made a positive impact on your environment or relationships. Describe the situation and the outcome.

_____
_____
_____

Chapter 13: Financial Stability

Section 1: Managing Your Money Wisely

Objective:

Understand the basics of budgeting and saving, recognize how important financial planning and financial literacy are, and learn how to open and manage checking and savings accounts effectively.

Introduction to Financial Stability

Objective:

Define financial stability and explain its importance in achieving long-term financial health.

Discussion: What is Financial Stability?

- **Definition of Financial Stability:** Financial stability means having control over your finances, which allows you to meet your current financial needs, save for the future, and handle unexpected expenses without falling into debt or financial hardship. It's about being secure and confident in your financial situation.

- **Impact on Personal Well-being:** Financial stability greatly affects your overall well-being. When you're financially stable, you experience less stress and anxiety about money, you have the freedom to make choices that improve your quality of life, and you're better prepared for the future.

- **Personal Experiences or Hypothetical Scenarios:**
  - **Example 1:** Imagine you're living paycheck to paycheck and an unexpected car repair comes up. Without savings, you'd have to borrow money or go into debt, which can be stressful.
  - **Example 2:** On the other hand, if you've been saving regularly, you have an emergency fund to cover the repair, leaving you stress-free and financially secure.

Section 2: Basics of Budgeting and Saving

Objective:

Learn the fundamental principles of budgeting and saving money.

1. **Budgeting Basics:**
   - **Income vs. Expenses:**
     - **Income:** This is the money you earn, like from a job, allowance, or gifts. It could be consistent (like a weekly allowance) or irregular (like money from a part-time job).
     - **Expenses:** These are the things you spend money on, such as food, clothes, entertainment, or school supplies. Expenses can be regular (like a monthly phone bill) or one-time purchases (like buying a new video game).
     - **Tracking Income and Expenses:**
       - Keeping a record of how much money you earn and where you spend it helps you understand your financial habits. It's important to track both so you can see if you're living within your means or overspending.
   - **Fixed vs. Variable Expenses:**
     - **Fixed Expenses:** These are expenses that don't change each month, such as rent, a phone bill, or a subscription service. You can predict these costs and plan for them.
     - **Variable Expenses:** These are costs that can change from month to month, like groceries, entertainment, or gas. These are more flexible, and you can adjust them based on your budget.
   - **Creating a Budget:**
     - Step 1: List your total income for the month.
     - Step 2: List all your fixed expenses.
     - Step 3: Estimate your variable expenses.

- Step 4: Subtract your total expenses from your total income to see what's left.
- Step 5: If you have money left over, decide how much to save or use for other goals. If your expenses are greater than your income, find ways to cut back on your variable expenses.

Section 3: Saving Strategies:

- **Setting Savings Goals:**
  - **Short-term Goals:** These are goals you want to achieve in the next few months to a year, like saving for a new phone or a trip.
  - **Medium-term Goals:** These are goals that might take a few years to reach, like saving for college or a car.
  - **Long-term Goals:** Goals that can take many years to achieve, like saving for a house or retirement.
- **Emergency Fund:**
  - **Importance:** An emergency fund is money set aside for unexpected expenses, such as a new tire or a broken window. Having this fund helps you avoid going into debt when surprises happen.
  - **How Much to Save:** A good rule of thumb is to save enough to cover 3-6 months of living expenses. Start small if you need to, and build it up over time.
- **Automating Savings:**
  - **Techniques for Consistent Saving:** Automating your savings means setting up automatic transfers a certain amount of money into your savings account every time you get paid. This way, you don't have to think about it, and your savings grow consistently.

- **Example:** If you earn $100 a week, you could set up an automatic transfer of $10 to your savings account each week. By the end of the year, you'd have $520 saved without even thinking about it.

Conclusion:

Understanding and practicing budgeting and saving are essential steps towards achieving financial stability. By managing your money wisely, setting goals, and saving consistently, you can build a secure financial future. Financial stability gives you peace of mind, freedom to make choices, and confidence in handling your financial life.

This lesson plan is designed to be clear and practical, helping students grasp the concepts of financial stability, budgeting, and saving in a way that's relatable to their daily lives. Encourage students to start small and stay consistent, as these habits will serve them well throughout their lives.

Worksheet 1: Understanding Financial Stability

Answer the following questions based on the material from Chapter 13.

1. Define the following terms:

    o **Financial Stability:**
    _____

    o **Impact on Personal Well-being:**
    _____

2. Discuss the impact of financial stability on personal well-being with the help of the provided scenarios.

a. Scenario 1: Imagine you have an unexpected expense and no savings. Describe how this might affect you.

_____

_____

b. Scenario 2: Imagine you have an emergency fund and encounter the same unexpected expense. Describe how this might affect you.

_____

_____

3. Why is financial stability important for achieving long-term financial health?

_____

_____

4. Provide two examples of how financial stability can improve your quality of life.

a.
_____

b.
_____

5. Reflect on a personal experience or a hypothetical situation where financial stability played a role. Describe the situation and the outcome.

_____
_____
_____
_____

Worksheet 2: Budgeting and Saving Strategies

Complete the exercises and questions below to apply budgeting and saving strategies.

1. Budgeting Basics:

a. List your sources of income and categorize them as consistent or irregular.

- Consistent Income:
  _____

- Irregular Income:
  _____

b. Identify and list three of your fixed expenses and three of your variable expenses.

- Fixed Expenses:
    1. _____
    2. _____
    3. _____
- Variable Expenses:
    1. _____
    2. _____
    3. _____

c. Create a simple budget by completing the following:

- Total Monthly Income: $
  _____

- Total Fixed Expenses: $
  _____

- Estimated Variable Expenses: $
  _____

- Remaining Amount: $ (Income - Fixed Expenses - Variable Expenses) _____

2. Saving Strategies:

a. Set one short-term, one medium-term, and one long-term savings goal.

- **Short-term Goal:**
  _____

- **Medium-term Goal:**
  _____

- **Long-term Goal:**
  _____

b. Calculate how much you should save each month to reach your short-term goal within the specified time frame.

- **Short-term Goal Amount: $**
  _____

- **Time Frame:**
  _____

- **Monthly Savings Needed: $ (Goal Amount / Number of Months)**
  _____

c. Explain the importance of having an emergency fund and suggest a strategy for building it.

- **Importance:**
  _____

- **Strategy:**
  _____

Chapter 14: Time Management

Section 1: Using Time Effectively

Time management skills help you use your time wisely to achieve your goals. In this chapter, we'll explore various techniques for prioritizing tasks, balancing responsibilities and leisure, and the importance of planning and scheduling.

1. Techniques for Prioritizing Tasks

When you have multiple tasks to complete, it's important to decide which ones are most important and should be done first. There are different techniques you can use to prioritize your tasks effectively.

ABC Method

- **Definition:** The ABC method is a simple technique where you categorize your tasks into three groups based on their importance:
    - **A tasks:** These are the most important tasks that must be done immediately or have the highest impact. They should be your top priority.
    - **B tasks:** These are important but not as urgent as A tasks. They should be done after all A tasks are completed.
    - **C tasks:** These are less important and can be done later if time permits. They usually have the least impact.
- **Guidelines for Categorizing Tasks:**
    - **Ask yourself:** What are the consequences of not completing this task today?
    - **Consider deadlines:** Is there a time limit for completing this task?
    - **Think about impact:** How does this task contribute to my overall goals?
- **Practical Exercise: Assigning Priorities to a Task List**
    - **Example Task List:**
        1. Study for tomorrow's math test.

2. Watch a new episode of your favorite show.
3. Finish the science project due next week.
4. Clean your room.
5. Help a friend with homework.

Section 2: Time Blocking

- **Definition and Benefits:**
    - Time Blocking is a where your day is divided into blocks of time, according to tasks or activities. This helps you focus better and ensures that you allocate enough time for important tasks.
    - Benefits: Increases productivity, reduces distractions, and helps you manage your time efficiently.
- **Creating Blocks of Focused Time for Specific Tasks:**
    - Identify your most important tasks and decide how much time you need for each.
    - Block out specific times during the day for each task.
    - Stick to your schedule and avoid multitasking during these blocks.
- **Practical Exercise: Time Blocking a Sample Day**
    - Example:
        - 8:00 AM - 9:00 AM: clean my bathroom.
        - 9:00 AM - 10:00 AM: get on zoom call with teacher.
        - 10:00 AM - 10:30 AM: do my homework.
        - 10:30 AM - 11:00 AM: call my mom.

Section 2: Balancing Responsibilities and Leisure

Balance between leisure and work is essential for maintaining your well-being and productivity. It's important to understand how to manage your responsibilities while still having time for relaxation and fun.

Understanding Work-Life Balance

- **Importance of Balancing Work and Personal Life:**
  - A healthy work-life balance ensures that you're not overburdened by work or school, allowing time for hobbies, relaxation, and socializing. It helps you stay refreshed and motivated.

- **Consequences of Imbalance:**
  - Stress: Constant work without breaks can lead to burnout and stress.
  - Decreased Productivity: When you're tired and stressed, your ability to focus and perform tasks efficiently decreases.
  - Health Issues: Lack of balance can cause mental, emotbonal, and physical issues, such as fatigue, anxiety, or depression.

Section 4: Setting Boundaries

- **Strategies for Defining Work and Personal Time:**
  - Set specific times for work and study, and stick to them.
  - Create a designated workspace to help mentally separate work from leisure.
  - Inform others of your schedule so they know when you're available for personal time.

- **Techniques for Avoiding Work Spillover into Personal Time:**
  - Avoid checking work emails or doing schoolwork during your personal time.
  - Use a planner or app to schedule your tasks and stick to the allotted time.
  - Practice saying "no" to additional tasks that could interfere with your personal time.

Section 5: Benefits of Planning

Planning is key to effective time management. It helps you organize your tasks, reduce stress, and make steady progress toward your goals.

Enhancing Productivity and Reducing Stress

- **How Planning Helps:**
    - By planning, you can make larger tasks smaller, and easier to keep up with to avoid rushing.
    - Knowing what to expect reduces anxiety and helps you feel more in control of your time.
- **Improving Long-Term and Short-Term Goal Achievement:**
    - Planning allows you to set clear, achievable and reachable goals. This keeps you motivated and focused on your objectives.

Long-Term Planning

- **Setting and Tracking Goals:**
    - Start by identifying your long-term goals (e.g., graduating, getting a job, etc.).
    - Break your goals into small, actionable trackable steps that are reachable over time.
- **Creating Action Plans and Timelines:**
    - For each goal, create an action plan that outlines what needs to be done and by when.
    - Use timelines to map out when you should complete each step, helping you stay on track.
- **Practical Exercise: Developing a Long-Term Plan for a Personal or Professional Project**
    - Example: Planning to get a driver's license.
        - Step 1: Enroll in a driving course (Deadline: 1st September).
        - Step 2: Complete the course and practice driving (Timeline: September - October).
        - Step 3: Schedule and pass the driving test (Target Date: End of October).

- **Step 4: Obtain your driver's license (Goal Completion: November).**

This curriculum provides a comprehensive approach to mastering time management skills, with practical exercises to reinforce learning.

Worksheet 1: Time Management Techniques

Complete the following exercises to practice using time management techniques.

Section 1: Prioritizing Tasks

1. Use the ABC Method to prioritize the following tasks. Categorize each task into A, B, or C based on its importance.

Task List:

- Study for tomorrow's math test.
- Watch a new episode of your favorite show.
- Finish the science project due next week.
- Clean your room.
- Help a friend with homework.

Priority Categories:

- A Tasks: _____
- B Tasks: _____
- C Tasks: _____

2. Explain why you categorized each task as A, B, or C.

- A Tasks: _____
- B Tasks: _____
- C Tasks: _____

Section 2: Time Blocking

1. **Create a time-blocked schedule for a sample day. Use the example provided to fill in your own time blocks for various tasks.**

Example:

- 8:00 AM - 9:00 AM: Clean my bathroom.
- 9:00 AM - 10:00 AM: Get on Zoom call with teacher.
- 10:00 AM - 10:30 AM: Do my homework.
- 10:30 AM - 11:00 AM: Call my mom.

Your Schedule:

- 8:00 AM - 9:00 AM: _____

- 9:00 AM - 10:00 AM: _____

- 10:00 AM - 10:30 AM: _____

- 10:30 AM - 11:00 AM: _____

- 11:00 AM - 12:00 PM: _____

2. **Describe one benefit of using time blocking in your schedule.**

_____

_____

Section 3: Balancing Responsibilities and Leisure

1. **List three responsibilities and three leisure activities you want to balance in your life.**

    o **Responsibilities:**

    1. _____
    2. _____
    3. _____

    o **Leisure Activities:**

    1. _____
    2. _____
    3. _____

2. **Explain why it is important to balance responsibilities with leisure time.**

    _____
    _____

Section 4: Setting Boundaries

1. **Identify two strategies you can use to set boundaries between work/study time and personal time.**

    o _____
    o _____

2. **Describe a technique you can use to avoid letting work spill over into your personal time.**

    _____
    _____
    _____

Worksheet 2: Planning and Goal Setting

Complete the following exercises to practice planning and setting goals.

Section 1: Short-Term and Long-Term Planning

1. Set one short-term goal and one long-term goal. For each goal, create a simple action plan and timeline.

Short-Term Goal:

- Goal:

  _____

- Action Plan:

    1. _____
    2. _____
    3. _____

- Timeline:

  _____

Long-Term Goal:

- Goal:

  _____

- Action Plan:

    1. _____
    2. _____
    3. _____

- Timeline:

  _____

2. Describe how planning helps in achieving long-term goals.

_____

_____

Chapter 15: Coping with Stress

Section 1: Healthy Ways to Manage Stress

Recognizing Stress and Its Sources

Understanding how to recognize stress and its sources is the first step in managing it effectively. This section will cover the different types of stress, common symptoms, and how to identify personal stressors.

1. Understanding Stress

Stress is your body's response to any demand or challenge. It can be positive (eustress) or negative (acute or chronic stress).

- Types of Stress:
    - Acute Stress: Short-term stress that arises quickly and is usually intense. For example, getting nervous before a test.
    - Chronic Stress: Long-term stress that persists over time. This can be due to ongoing issues like financial problems or an unhealthy relationship.
    - Eustress (Positive Stress): Stress that is motivating and helps you perform better. An example would be the excitement you feel when preparing for a competition.
- Common Symptoms of Stress:
    - Physical: Headaches, fatigue, upset stomach, muscle tension, and rapid heartbeat.
    - Emotional: Anxiety, irritability, sadness, or mood swings.
    - Behavioral: Changes in eating habits, sleep disturbances, withdrawal from social activities, or increased use of alcohol or drugs.

Section 2: Identifying Stress Triggers

Stress triggers are the situations, people, or events that cause you to feel stressed. Identifying these triggers helps you manage your stress more effectively.

- **Common Sources of Stress:**
  - **Work/School:** Deadlines, exams, workload, or conflicts with peers or colleagues.
  - **Relationships:** Arguments with family or friends, relationship issues, or social pressures.
  - **Finances:** Money problems, debt, or job instability.
  - **Daily Hassles:** Traffic, long commutes, household chores, or unexpected events.

Section 3: Techniques for Identifying Personal Stressors:

- **Self-reflection:** Think about situations that cause you to feel stressed.
- **Stress Journal:** Write down the events or situations that trigger your stress, how you felt, and how you responded.
- **Practical Exercise: Keeping a Stress Journal**
  - **Instructions:** For one week, record any situation that makes you feel stressed. Note the date, time, event, your feelings, and how you handled it. At the end of the week, review your journal to identify patterns or common triggers.
  - When feeling stressed do this for about 15 minutes. Focus on your breathing and let go of any distracting thoughts.

1. Physical Activity

Exercise is one of the most effective ways to manage stress.

- **Benefits of Exercise on Stress Reduction:**
  - Physical activity reduces stress hormones, increases the production of endorphins, which are natural mood lifters
- **Types of Stress-Relief Exercises:**
  - **Aerobic Exercises:** Activities like running, swimming, or cycling that increase your heart rate.

- **Yoga:** Combines physical postures, breathing exercises, and meditation to reduce stress and improve flexibility.
- **Stretching:** Simple stretches can release muscle tension and improve circulation.

- **Practical Exercise: Designing a Personalized Exercise Plan**
  - **Instructions:** Create a weekly 30-45 minute at least three times a week exercise plan.

1. **Healthy Eating and Hydration** Choose a good healthy diet that you can continue and won't quit on.

- **Impact of Nutrition on Stress Levels:**
  - Eating a balanced diet helps stabilize your blood sugar, improve your mood, and keep your energy levels steady.
- **Ways to maintain a balanced Diet:**
  - Eat plenty of fruits, lean protein, fresh vegetables, and whole grains.
  - Avoid excessive caffeine, sugar, and processed foods.
  - Drink plenty of water throughout the day to stay hydrated.
- **Practical Exercise: Creating a Stress-Reducing Meal Plan**
  - **Instructions:** Plan your meals for one day, including breakfast, lunch, dinner, and snacks. Focus on including foods that are rich in vitamins, minerals, and antioxidants, and avoid foods that may increase stress.

1. **Time Management and Organization**

Time management helps to reduce stress by keeping you on top of your tasks and responsibilities.

- **Reducing Stress Through Effective Time Management:**
  - Plan each day thoroughly prioritizing your tasks, to help create more free time for relaxation.

1. **Relaxation Techniques**

Learning how to relax your body and mind is essential for managing stress.

- **Introduction to Relaxation Techniques:**
    - Aromatherapy: lavender, stress relief, etc.
    - Listening to Calming Music: Soft music or nature sounds can help lower stress levels and promote relaxation.
- **Practical Exercise: Practicing a Relaxation Technique**
    - Instructions: Choose one relaxation technique and practice it for 10 minutes. Pay attention to how your body feels before and after the exercise.

1. Social Support

Having a strong support network is vital for managing stress.

- **Social Support in Stress Management:**
    - Talking to friends, family, or a counselor.
- **Building and Maintaining a Support Network:**
    - Join clubs, groups, or online communities that interest you.
    - Don't hesitate to ask for help when you need it.

1. Importance of Self-Care

Self-care helps you maintain physical, emotional, and mental well-being.

1. Understanding Self-Care

Self-care involves activities that help you take care of your health and well-being.

- **Definition and Importance of Self-Care:**
    - Self-Care: All deliberate activities that help you to smile, be happy and relax.
- **Types of Self-Care:**
    - Physical: Activities that improve your physical health, like exercise, sleep, and nutrition.

- **Emotional:** Activities that help you process and express your emotions.
- **Mental:** Activities that challenge and stimulate your mind.

1. **Incorporating Self-Care into Daily Life**

Integrating self-care into your routine helps you stay balanced and manage stress more effectively.

- **Strategies for Integrating Self-Care Practices into a Busy Schedule:**
    - Schedule time for self-care, even if it's just 10-15 minutes a day.
    - Combine self-care with daily activities, like listening to music while cooking or taking a walk during your lunch break.
    - Be consistent and treat self-care as a non-negotiable part of your day.
- **Examples of Self-Care Activities:**
    - **Hobbies:** Painting, knitting, gardening, or playing a musical instrument.
    - **Relaxation:** Taking a bubble bath, meditating, or practicing deep breathing.
    - **Personal Time:** Spending time alone to recharge, reading, or taking a nap.
- **Practical Exercise: Creating a Self-Care Plan**
    - **Instructions:** Write down three self-care activities you enjoy and plan how you will incorporate them into your weekly routine. Make sure these activities are realistic and achievable given your schedule.

1. **Setting Boundaries and Saying No**

Helps you protect your time and energy.

- **Setting Boundaries and Protecting Your Personal Time:**
    - Boundaries allow you to say no to things that drain your energy or time, helping you focus on what's most important.

- **Techniques for Saying No and Managing Expectations:**
    - Be Assertive: Clearly and politely say no when you need to.
    - Offer Alternatives: If you can't do something, suggest a different way to help.
    - Explain Your Reasons: You don't have to justify yourself, but offering a brief explanation can help others understand your decision.
- **Practical Exercise: Role-Playing Boundary-Setting Scenarios**
    - Instructions: Pair up with a classmate. One of you will play the role of someone asking for a favor, while the other practices saying no and setting a boundary. Switch roles after a few minutes.

1. Seeking Professional Help

Sometimes, managing stress on your own isn't enough, and seeking professional help is necessary.

- **Recognizing When Professional Help Is Needed:**
    - If stress is overwhelming and affecting your daily life, it might be time to seek help from a professional.
- **Types of Professionals:**
    - Therapists: Trained to help you understand and manage your emotions and behavior.
    - Counselors: Provide guidance on personal or psychological issues.
    - Coaches: Help you set and achieve personal goals.
- **Information on Finding and Accessing Mental Health Resources:**
    - Hotlines: National Suicide Prevention Lifeline, Crisis Text Line.
    - Online Therapy: Services like BetterHelp or Talkspace offer remote therapy options.
    - Local Resources: Look for local mental health centers or ask your doctor for a referral.

This lesson plan offers a comprehensive approach to understanding and managing stress, with practical exercises that help students apply what they've learned.

Worksheet 1: Recognizing and Managing Stress

Complete the following exercises to identify stressors and practice stress management techniques.

Section 1: Understanding Stress

1. **Define each type of stress below and provide an example for each.**

    - Acute Stress:
        - **Definition:**

        _____

        - **Example:**

        _____

    - Chronic Stress:
        - **Definition:**

        _____

        - **Example:**

        _____

    - Eustress (Positive Stress):
        - **Definition:**

        _____

        - **Example:**

        _____

2. **List three common symptoms of stress. For each symptom, provide an example of how it might affect you.**

    - Physical Symptom:
        - **Example:**

        _____

- Emotional Symptom:
    - Example:
      _____

- Behavioral Symptom:
    - Example:
      _____

Section 2: Identifying Stress Triggers

1. **Think about your own life and identify one stress trigger from each of the following categories.**

   - Work/School:
       - Example:
         _____

   - Relationships:
       - Example:
         _____

   - Finances:
       - Example:
         _____

   - Daily Hassles:
       - Example:
         _____

Section 3: Stress-Relief Strategies

1. **Create a personalized exercise plan. Include at least three different types of exercises and their frequency.**

   - Exercise 1:
     _____

   - Frequency:
     _____

- Exercise 2: _____
- Frequency: _____
- Exercise 3: _____
- Frequency: _____

2. **Plan a stress-reducing meal for one day. Include breakfast, lunch, dinner, and snacks. Focus on including nutritious foods.**
    - Breakfast: _____
    - Lunch: _____
    - Dinner: _____
    - Snacks: _____

3. **Choose one relaxation technique and practice it for 10 minutes. Describe how it made you feel before and after.**
    - Technique Used: _____
    - Before: _____
    - After: _____

Worksheet 2: Implementing Stress Management Techniques

Use the following exercises to develop and implement effective stress management strategies.

Section 1: Creating a Self-Care Plan

1. Write down three self-care activities you enjoy and plan how you will incorporate them into your weekly routine.

    - Activity 1: _____

        - Plan: _____

    - Activity 2: _____

        - Plan: _____

    - Activity 3: _____

        - Plan: _____

2. Explain how incorporating self-care activities into your routine helps you manage stress.

Section 2: Setting Boundaries

1. Role-Play Scenario: Practice setting boundaries in the following situations. Write down how you would respond.

    - Scenario 1: A friend asks you to help with a project that you don't have time for.

- Response:
  _____

- Scenario 2: Your workload has increased and you need to say no to additional responsibilities.
  - Response:
    _____

2. Describe a technique you can use to manage expectations and avoid work spillover into your personal time.

_____

_____

Section 3: Seeking Professional Help

1. Identify when it might be necessary to seek professional help for managing stress. List two signs that indicate professional help might be needed.
   - Sign 1:
     _____
   - Sign 2:
     _____

2. Provide two types of professionals who can help with stress management and describe what they do.
   - Professional 1:
     _____
     - Description:
       _____
   - Professional 2:
     _____
     - Description:
       _____

Chapter 16: Conflict Resolution - Handling Conflicts Constructively

Objective:

To offer learners skills and strategies needed to resolve conflicts peacefully, understand the importance of compromise and empathy, and utilize effective communication techniques in conflict resolution.

Section 1: Introduction to Conflict Resolution

Definition of Conflict:

- A conflict is a disagreement or clash between ideas, principles, or people that comes from differences in goals, needs, values, or perceptions.
- Common causes of conflicts include:
    - Miscommunication or lack of communication.
    - Differences in values or beliefs.
    - Competing interests or goals.
    - Personality clashes.
    - Perceived unfairness or injustice.

Why Conflict Resolution is Important:

- Unresolved conflicts can lead to:
    - Damaged relationships: Conflicts can create distance and resentment between people.
    - Decreased productivity: In a work or school setting, conflicts can disrupt teamwork and focus.
    - Personal stress and anxiety: Carrying unresolved conflict can lead to emotional and mental strain.

Steps to Resolve Conflicts Peacefully

Step 1: Identify Where the Conflict is Coming From

- Techniques for recognizing the root cause:

- Ask yourself or others what specifically caused the disagreement.
- Look for patterns or recurring issues.
- Reflect on any unmet needs or expectations that might be fueling the conflict.

- Activity:
  - Role-playing: In pairs, one student presents a conflict scenario, and the other identifies the root cause. They then switch roles.

Step 2: Acknowledge the Conflict

- Importance of admitting that a conflict exists:
  - Denying or ignoring a conflict often makes it worse. Acknowledging it is the first step toward resolution.
- Activity:
  - Reflection exercise: Students write about a time when they acknowledged a conflict and how it helped (or could have helped) resolve it.

Step 3: Express Concerns Calmly

- Strategies for communicating feelings and needs without escalating the conflict:
  - Use "I" statements (e.g., "I feel... when... because...").
  - Avoid blame or accusations.
  - Stay focused on the issue, not the person.
- Activity:
  - Practice using "I" statements: Students practice with a partner, focusing on how to express their concerns calmly.

Step 4: Listen Actively

- Techniques for active listening:
  - Give full attention to the speaker.
  - Reflect back what you heard (e.g., "So what you're saying is...").

- Ask clarifying questions if needed.
- Activity:
  - Listening exercises: Students practice reflecting back what they hear in pairs and then discuss how it felt to be truly listened to.

Step 5: Explore Solutions Together

- **Brainstorming possible solutions:**
  - Encourage creative thinking.
  - Evaluate each solution's pros and cons together.
- Activity:
  - Group discussions: Present a conflict scenario and have groups brainstorm and evaluate potential solutions.

Step 6: Agree on a Solution and Implement It

- Developing a plan of action:
  - Choose a solution that everyone agrees on.
  - Outline the steps to implement the solution.
- Activity:
  - Conflict resolution plan: Students develop a plan for a given scenario and discuss how they would implement it.

Step 7: Follow-Up

- Importance of reviewing the resolution:
  - Ensure the solution is working and make adjustments if needed.
- Activity:
  - Role-play follow-up meetings: Students simulate a follow-up meeting to check on how well the resolution is working.

Section 2: Importance of Compromise and Understanding

Definition of Compromise:

- **A compromise is when both parties in a conflict agree to give up something to reach a mutually acceptable solution.**

Benefits of Compromise:

- Sustainable outcomes: Compromises often lead to more durable solutions because both sides feel heard and respected.
- Positive relationships: Compromising shows a willingness to work together and can strengthen relationships.

Understanding Different Perspectives:

- Seeing the conflict from the other person's point of view can help in finding a fair solution.
- Activity:
    - Perspective-taking exercises: Students switch roles in a scenario and try to articulate the other party's viewpoint.

Section 3: The Role of Communication in Conflict Resolution

Effective Communication Skills:

- Verbal Communication:
    - Use clear, concise, and respectful language.
    - Focus on the issue, not the person.
- Non-Verbal Communication:
    - Pay attention to body language, facial expressions, and tone of voice, as they can convey as much as words.
- Barriers to Effective Communication:
    - Common barriers include assumptions, prejudices, and misinterpretations. It's important to clarify and verify understanding.

Worksheet 1: Understanding and Resolving Conflict

Complete the exercises to deepen your understanding of conflict resolution.

Section 1: Introduction to Conflict

1. **Define Conflict:**
    - **Definition of Conflict:**
      _____

    - **Common Causes of Conflict:**
        - Cause 1:
          _____

        - Cause 2:
          _____

        - Cause 3:
          _____

        - Cause 4:
          _____

        - Cause 5:
          _____

2. **Why is Conflict Resolution Important?**
    - List two negative impacts of unresolved conflicts on relationships and productivity:
        - Impact 1:
          _____

        - Impact 2:
          _____

Section 2: Steps to Resolve Conflicts Peacefully

1. **Identify the Conflict:**
    - Scenario:
      _____

- Identify the Root Cause:
  - Ask yourself or others:
    _____
  - Look for patterns:
    _____
  - Reflect on unmet needs or expectations:
    _____

Activity: Role-Playing

- Scenario Provided:
  _____
- Root Cause Identified:
  _____

2. Acknowledge the Conflict:
   - Reflection Exercise: Write about a time when acknowledging a conflict helped (or could have helped) resolve it.
     - Description:
       _____
     - Outcome:
       _____

3. Express Concerns Calmly:
   - Using "I" Statements Practice:
     - Situation:
       _____
     - "I" Statement Example:
       _____
     - How did it feel to use this method?:
       _____

4. Listen Actively:
   - Active Listening Techniques Practice:

- **Reflecting Back Exercise:**
  _____

- **Clarifying Questions:**
  _____

- **Discussion on Listening Experience:**
  _____

5. **Explore Solutions Together:**
   - **Brainstorming Exercise:**
     - **Conflict Scenario:**
       _____

     - **Potential Solutions:**
       _____

     - **Pros and Cons of Each Solution:**
       _____

6. **Agree on a Solution and Implement It:**
   - **Conflict Resolution Plan:**
     - **Chosen Solution:**
       _____

     - **Steps to Implement the Solution:**
       _____

     - **How will you ensure its effectiveness?:**
       _____

Worksheet 2: Compromise, Understanding, and Communication

Complete the following exercises to practice compromise, understanding different perspectives, and effective communication.

Section 1: Importance of Compromise and Understanding

1. **Definition and Benefits of Compromise:**
    - **Definition of Compromise:**
      _____
    - **Benefits:**
        - **Benefit 1:**
          _____
        - **Benefit 2:**
          _____

2. **Understanding Different Perspectives:**
    - **Perspective-Taking Exercise:**
        - **Scenario:**
          _____
        - **Your Perspective:**
          _____
        - **Other Party's Perspective:**
          _____
        - **Articulate Other Party's Viewpoint:**
          _____

Section 2: The Role of Communication in Conflict Resolution

1. **Effective Communication Skills:**
    - **Verbal Communication:**
        - Use clear, concise, and respectful language.

- **Example:**
  _____

- o **Non-Verbal Communication:**
  - **Pay attention to body language, facial expressions, and tone of voice.**
  - **Example:**
    _____

2. **Barriers to Effective Communication:**
   - o **List and Describe Common Barriers:**
     - **Barrier 1:**
       _____
       - **Description:**
         _____
     - **Barrier 2:**
       _____
       - **Description:**
         _____
       - _____
   - o **Techniques for Overcoming Barriers:**
     - **Technique 1:**
       _____
     - **Technique 2:**
       _____

Chapter 17: Civic Responsibility - Being an Active and Responsible Citizen

Objective:

Students will understand the concept of civic responsibility, its historical significance, and the importance of community service and civic engagement in society.

Section 1: Definition of Civic Responsibility

Civic Responsibility:

- **Definition:** Civic responsibility refers to the duties and obligations each citizen has to society. It involves being an active participant in the community and working towards the common good.

- **Examples:**
    - Voting in elections.
    - Volunteering for local charities or organizations.
    - Following laws and regulations.
    - Respecting the rights of others.
    - Participating in community clean-ups or public service initiatives.

Section 2: Historical Perspectives on Civic Engagement

Historical Examples of Civic Engagement:

- **Ancient Greece:** The concept of democracy in Athens where citizens were expected to participate in decision-making.

- **Civil Rights Movement:** Activism during the 1960s in the United States where citizens fought for equality and justice.

- **Women's Suffrage:** The fight for women's right to vote, showcasing the importance of civic participation in changing laws and society.

Why Historical Perspective Matters:

- Understanding the past helps us appreciate the freedoms and responsibilities we have today. Civic engagement has always played a crucial role in shaping societies and driving progress.

Section 3: Overview of the Benefits of Active Citizenship

Benefits of Active Citizenship:

- **Personal Growth:**
    - Develops leadership skills.
    - Builds a sense of purpose and fulfillment.
    - Encourages lifelong learning and awareness of societal issues.
- **Societal Impact:**
    - Strengthens communities by addressing local needs.
    - Promotes social justice and equality.
    - Ensures that the voices of all citizens are heard, contributing to a more inclusive society.

Section 4: Importance of Community Involvement

Objective:

Explore various ways students can contribute positively to society through different forms of civic engagement.

Benefits of Community Involvement for Personal Growth and Societal Impact

Personal Growth:

- **Skill Development:** Volunteering and community service contribute to developmental skills like communicating effectively, teamwork, and problem-solving.
- **Sense of Belonging:** Being involved in community helps people get connected and network with others.
- **Increased Empathy:** Engaging with different people and communities increases understanding and empathy.

Societal Impact:

- **Strengthening Communities:** Community involvement addresses local issues, such as poverty, education, and environmental concerns.
- **Creating Positive Change:** Active citizens can influence policy and drive societal progress by participating in civic activities.

Volunteering and Community Service Opportunities

Ways to Get Involved:

- **Local Charities and Nonprofits:**
    - **Examples:** Food banks, animal shelters, hospitals, and educational programs.
    - **Activity:** Students can research and present a local organization where they can volunteer.
- **School-Based Service:**
    - **Examples:** Joining student councils, participating in school clean-ups, or tutoring peers.
- **Neighborhood Initiatives:**
    - **Examples:** Organizing or participating in community clean-up events, planting trees, or helping neighbors in need.

Section 5: Advocacy and Activism: How to Get Involved

Understanding Advocacy and Activism:

- **Advocacy:** Speaking out on behalf of others to influence policy or bring attention to important issues.
    - **Examples:** Writing letters to elected officials, participating in awareness campaigns, or using social media to raise awareness.
- **Activism:** Taking direct action to bring about social or political change.
    - **Examples:** Protesting, organizing events, or joining movements that align with personal beliefs.

How Students Can Get Involved:

- **Identify a Cause:** Encourage students to think about what matters to them in the community, like quality education, equal rights, keeping the community clean, stopping homelessness.
- **Take Action:** Students can start a campaign, join a local advocacy group, or use social media to spread awareness.

Section 6: Supporting Local Businesses and Organizations

Why Support Local:

- **Economic Benefits:** Supporting local businesses keeps money within the community, boosting the local economy.
- **Community Development:** Local businesses often support local events and charities, fostering a sense of community.

Ways to Support:

- **Shop Locally:** Choose local stores over big chains when possible.
- **Spread the Word:** Encourage friends and family to support local businesses through word-of-mouth or social media.
- **Participate in Local Events:** Attend farmers' markets, community fairs, and other local events to show support.

Section 7: Participating in Local Government and Public Affairs

Understanding Local Government:

- **Roles:** Local government includes mayors, city councils, and school boards that make decisions affecting the community.
- **Why Participation Matters:** Being involved ensures that citizens' needs and concerns are represented.

How to Get Involved:

- **Attend Town Meetings:** These are open to the public and a great way to learn about local issues.
- **Vote in Local Elections:** Encourage students to understand the importance of voting, even in local elections.

- **Volunteer for Campaigns:** Students can volunteer for local candidates or causes they believe in.

Section 7: Understanding Individual Rights and Freedoms

What Are Individual Rights?

- **Basic Freedoms:** These include freedom of speech, religion, and the right to a fair trial.
- **Responsibilities:** With rights come responsibilities, such as respecting others' rights and obeying laws.

How to Exercise and Protect Your Rights Responsibly:

- **Stay Informed:** Know your rights and understand current events that may affect them.
- **Respect Others:** Exercise your rights in ways that do not infringe on the rights of others.
- **Stand Up for What's Right:** When rights are threatened, use peaceful and lawful means to defend them, such as petitions, protests, or legal action.

This information should help your students grasp the significance of civic responsibility and community involvement, empowering them to become active and responsible citizens.

Worksheet 1: Understanding Civic Responsibility

Complete the following exercises to enhance your understanding of civic responsibility and how you can be an active and responsible citizen.

Section 1: Definition of Civic Responsibility

1. Define Civic Responsibility:
   - **Definition:**
     _____
   - **Examples of Civic Responsibility:** (List at least three examples.)
     - Example 1:
       _____
     - Example 2:
       _____
     - Example 3:
       _____

2. Why is Civic Responsibility Important?
   - **Explanation:**
     _____
   - **Personal Impact:**
     _____
   - **Community Impact:**
     _____

Section 2: Historical Perspectives on Civic Engagement

1. Historical Examples:
   - **Civil Rights Movement:** What was the significance of civic engagement during this period?
     - Significance:
       _____
   - **Women's Suffrage:** How did the fight for women's right to vote impact society?

- Impact:
  _____

2. **Why Understanding Historical Perspectives Matters:**
   o **Explanation:**
   _____

Section 3: Benefits of Active Citizenship

1. **Personal Growth Benefits:**
   o **Benefit 1:**
   _____
   o **Benefit 2:**
   _____
   o **Benefit 3:**
   _____

2. **Societal Impact Benefits:**
   o **Benefit 1:**
   _____
   o **Benefit 2:**
   _____
   o **Benefit 3:**
   _____

Section 4: Community Involvement

1. **Ways to Get Involved:**
   o **Local Charities and Nonprofits: Research and list one local organization where you can volunteer.**
     - **Organization:**
     _____
     - **Type of Service:**
     _____

- **School-Based Service:** List one way you can contribute to your school community.
    - **Activity:** _____

- **Neighborhood Initiatives:** Describe a neighborhood initiative you could participate in.
    - **Initiative:** _____

2. **Benefits of Community Involvement:**
    - **Personal Growth Benefits:** _____
    - **Societal Impact Benefits:** _____

Worksheet 2: Advocacy, Local Government, and Individual Rights

Complete the following exercises to understand advocacy, local government involvement, and individual rights.

Section 1: Advocacy and Activism

1. Understanding Advocacy:

    o **Definition of Advocacy:**
    _____

    o **Examples of Advocacy: (List two examples.)**

        - Example 1:
        _____

        - Example 2:
        _____

2. Understanding Activism:

    o **Definition of Activism:**
    _____

    o **Examples of Activism: (List two examples.)**

        - Example 1:
        _____

        - Example 2:
        _____

3. How to Get Involved:

    o **Identify a Cause: Choose a cause that matters to you and describe why it is important.**

        - Cause:
        _____

        - Reason:
        _____

- Take Action: Outline one action you can take to support this cause.
  - Action: _____

Section 2: Supporting Local Businesses and Organizations

1. **Why Support Local:**
   - Economic Benefits: _____
   - Community Development: _____

2. **Ways to Support Local:**
   - Shop Locally: Describe one way you can support local businesses.
     - Example: _____
   - Spread the Word: How can you encourage others to support local businesses?
     - Method: _____
   - Participate in Local Events: List one local event you can attend to show support.
     - Event: _____

Section 3: Participating in Local Government and Public Affairs

1. **Understanding Local Government:**
   - Roles of Local Government: Briefly describe the role of a mayor, city council, and school board.
     - Mayor: _____

- City Council:
  _____

- School Board:
  _____

2. How to Get Involved:

    o Attend Town Meetings: Explain why attending town meetings is beneficial.

    - Explanation:
      _____

    o Vote in Local Elections: Why is voting in local elections important?

    - Explanation:
      _____

    o Volunteer for Campaigns: Describe one way you can volunteer for a local candidate or cause.

    - Method:
      _____

Section 4: Understanding Individual Rights and Freedoms

1. What Are Individual Rights?:

    o Basic Freedoms: List three basic freedoms guaranteed by individual rights.

    - Freedom 1:
      _____

    - Freedom 2:
      _____

    - Freedom 3:
      _____

2. How to Exercise and Protect Your Rights Responsibly:

    o Stay Informed: Describe one way to stay informed about your rights.

- **Method:**
  _____

- **Respect Others:** Explain how to exercise your rights while respecting others.
  - **Explanation:**
    _____

- **Stand Up for What's Right:** Provide an example of a peaceful and lawful way to defend your rights.
  - **Example:**
    _____

Definitions

Active Listening - Communication that involves totally concentrating on the speaker, understanding their message, responding thoughtfully, and remembering what was said. Active listening is a must to have effective communication and conflict resolution.

Acute Stress - Short-term stress that arises quickly and is intense but usually resolves quickly. Examples include feeling nervous before a test or presentation.

Advocacy - The act of speaking out on behalf of others to influence policy or bring attention to important issues.

Activism - Direct action taken to bring about social or political change, such as protesting, organizing events, or joining movements.

Automating Savings - Automatic transfers to your checking or savings account.

Assertiveness - The ability to express one's thoughts, feelings, and needs confidently and respectfully, without being aggressive. Assertiveness is crucial for maintaining personal boundaries and saying no when necessary.

Bacterial STDs - Sexually transmitted diseases caused by bacteria, such as Chlamydia, Gonorrhea, and Syphilis. These infections are typically treatable with antibiotics.

Boundaries - Limits or rules that individuals set to protect their well-being and personal space. They tell you what others or willing to or not to accept.

Budgeting - A process of creating a plan to manage your income and expenses. This is where you track your earnings and how much you spend, setting aside money for savings, and ensuring that your expenses do not exceed your income.

Bullying - Intentional, aggressive behavior typically repeated over time, aimed at harming or controlling the target.

Career Advancement - The process of personal or professional advancement in one's career, often through promotions, increased responsibilities, or acquiring new skills.

Chronic Stress - Long-term stress that persists over time, often due to ongoing issues like financial problems or a difficult relationship.

Civic Engagement - Involvement in activities intended to influence public policy or address issues of public concern, such as being a volunteer, voting, or doing community service.

Civic Responsibility - The duties and obligations each citizen has to society, which involves being an active participant in the community and working towards the common good.

Compromise - A compromise is when both parties in a conflict agree to give up something to reach a mutually acceptable solution.

Comprehensive Sex Education - An educational approach that provides students with knowledge about sexual health, contraception, healthy relationships, and the consequences of early pregnancy. It is intended to empower individuals to make informed decisions about their sexual health.

Conflict - A conflict is a disagreement or clash between ideas, principles, or people that arises from differences in goals, needs, values, or perceptions.

Conflict Resolution - Resolving disagreements between individuals or groups peacefully and constructively, often through communication, compromise, and understanding.

Consent - A clear, enthusiastic, and ongoing agreement between partners to engage in specific activities. Consent must be given and can be taken away at any time.

Critical Thinking - Analyze information and arguments in a logical and objective manner to form a reasoned judgment.

Demographics - Statistical data relating to the population and particular groups within it. In the context of teenage pregnancy, demographics may include age, ethnicity, geographic location, and socioeconomic status.

Dating Violence - A pattern of controlling, abusive, or aggressive behavior in a romantic relationship. This can include physical, emotional, verbal, or sexual abuse.

Empathy - Understanding other's feelings or putting yourself in someone else's shoes. Empathy is important in communication as it helps build trust and understanding between individuals.

Eustress (Positive Stress) - A type of stress that is beneficial and motivates you to perform better. For example, the excitement before a competition or challenge.

Financial Stability - The ability to manage your finances in a way that you can meet your current needs, save for future goals, and handle unexpected expenses without falling into debt or financial hardship. It involves having control over your financial situation and being confident in your financial security.

Goal Setting - The process of identifying measurable and achievable objectives that guide actions and decisions.

Higher Education - Post-secondary education that includes undergraduate, graduate, and doctoral programs offered by colleges and universities.

Income - Money you receive, such as from a job, allowance, or gifts. It can be consistent (like a salary) or irregular (like freelance work).

Individual Rights - The basic freedoms and protections that every citizen is entitled to, such as freedom of speech, religion, and the right to a fair trial.

"I" Statements - A communication method where the speaker expresses their feelings and needs without blaming others, usually in the format of "I feel... when... because...".

Long-Term Goals - Objectives that require a longer time to achieve, typically spanning several years. They offer a vision for the future and guide sustained efforts.

Menstrual Hygiene - Practices related to managing menstruation, including the use of sanitary products and maintaining cleanliness to prevent infection.

Mindset - Established attitudes an individual has about their beliefs, abilities and potential for growth.

Mutual Respect - Treating your partner with consideration and valuing their feelings and opinions. Mutual respect is fundamental to a healthy and respectful relationship.

Non-Verbal Communication - The transmission of messages or information without the use of words that may come through eye contact, body movement, and facial expressions.

Peer Pressure - Positive or negative influence by peers on an individual to conform to the group's expectations and behaviors. Peer pressure oftentimes is a significant factor in teenagers' decisions regarding sex, substance use, and other behaviors.

Persistence - The continued effort to achieve a goal despite challenges, setbacks, or obstacles. Persistence is crucial for overcoming difficulties and maintaining motivation.

Personal Hygiene - Practices that individuals engage in to maintain cleanliness and promote health, including bathing, brushing teeth, and washing hands.

Positive Self-Talk - Speaking to yourself in an inspirational and encouraging manner. It involves using affirmations and constructive inner dialogue to boost self-esteem and motivation.

Prevalence - The frequency or rate at which a particular event or condition occurs in a population. In this context, it refers to the rate of teenage pregnancies or births among a specific age group.

Problem-Solving - Finding solutions to complex issues.

Red Flags - Warning signs indicating that a relationship may be unhealthy or abusive. Examples include extreme jealousy, controlling behavior, and verbal insults.

Resilience - When you are able to bounce back from serious issues, stress, and challenges. It involves adaptability, perseverance, and maintaining a positive outlook despite difficulties.

Saving - Setting aside money you have made for future later use. Saving helps you prepare for emergencies, achieve financial goals, and build financial security.

Self-Care - Self-care refers to actions and practices that individuals engage in regularly to maintain and improve their physical, emotional, and mental health.

Self-Efficacy - How much you believe in yourself to succeed in life and to feel accomplished with your own progress.

Self-Esteem - How much individuals appreciate and like themselves.

Self-Love - Taking care of your own needs and not sacrificing well-being to please others. It involves self-acceptance, self-compassion, and the pursuit of personal growth and happiness.

Self-Reflection - Self-reflection is the process of introspection, where individuals examine their thoughts, feelings, and behaviors to gain deeper self-awareness.

SMART Goals - An acronym for Specific, Measurable, Achievable, Relevant, and Time-Bound goals. SMART goals are designed to provide clear and attainable objectives that can be tracked and accomplished within a specified timeframe.

Short-Term Goals - Objectives that can be achieved within a relatively short period, usually within a year. These goals provide immediate direction and quick wins.

Skill Specialization - Gaining expertise in a specific area or field, which makes one more competitive in the job market.

Socioeconomic Factors - Social and economic characteristics that influence an individual's or group's behavior and outcomes, such as income level, education, and access to resources.

Stress - A physical and emotional response to a demand or challenge. It can be positive (motivating, known as eustress) or negative (overwhelming, known as acute or chronic stress).

Stress Triggers - Situations, events, or people that cause you to feel stressed. Knowing these triggers can help someone reduce their stress.

Support Systems - Networks of people, resources, or organizations that provide emotional, social, or practical assistance during times of need.

Time Management - Planning and controlling the amount of time you spend on certain activities to increase efficiency and productivity.

Unconditional Love - Love that is given without conditions or expectations. It involves accepting and caring for someone without needing them to meet specific criteria.

Values - Core beliefs and principles that guide an individual's behavior and decisions. Values influence how people view the world and interact with others.

Victimization - The process of being harmed, abused, or made to feel powerless. It can occur in various contexts, including bullying, sexual abuse, and domestic violence.

Work-Life Balance - The ability to effectively manage work responsibilities and personal life, ensuring neither area is neglected or overwhelms the other.

Youth Empowerment - Initiatives and practices designed to give young people the skills, confidence, and opportunities to make decisions and influence their own lives and communities.

References

2023 Report on STDs: Centers for Disease Control and Prevention (CDC). (2023). *Sexually Transmitted Disease Surveillance 2023*. Retrieved from CDC STD Surveillance 2023

2022 Report on STDs: Centers for Disease Control and Prevention (CDC). (2022). *Sexually Transmitted Disease Surveillance 2022*. Retrieved from CDC STD Surveillance 2022

2023 Report on Teenage Pregnancy: Centers for Disease Control and Prevention (CDC). (2023). *Teen Births*. Retrieved from CDC Teen Births 2023

2022 Report on Teenage Pregnancy: Centers for Disease Control and Prevention (CDC). (2022). *Teen Births*. Retrieved from CDC Teen Births 2022

Dr. Charmaine Marie, Ed.D., is a devoted advocate for youth, blending her love for writing with a profound passion for empowering young minds. As a diverse author, Dr. Charmaine Marie crafts books designed to inspire and uplift, providing young readers with the tools to build a solid foundation in life, self-love, and greatness. Her writing is a reflection of her unwavering commitment to nurturing the potential within each young person, guiding them toward a future marked by success and fulfillment.

While she wears many hats—Realtor®, Executive Director of Real L.O.V.E., and a dedicated Navy Reserve Machinist Mate—Dr. Charmaine Marie's first love is the youth and their outcomes in life. She pours her heart into creating works that resonate with young readers, encouraging them to embrace their unique strengths and pursue their dreams with confidence. Through her books, Dr. Charmaine Marie hopes to leave a lasting, positive imprint on the next generation, helping them navigate their journey with resilience, self-respect, and a sense of purpose.

www.ingramcontent.com/pod-product-compliance
Lightning Source LLC
Chambersburg PA
CBHW050454110426
42743CB00017B/3357